Foreword

Our Holy Father, Pope Bened— ————————————————— —n *Caritatis*, reminds us that 'the —————————————————— be firmly believed, devoutly celeb————

Sharing in His Life is an opportu—————— —————————luals to reflect on their celebration of the Eucharist. Over the next six weeks you will be invited to focus on what we are called to engage with when we are at Mass and to prayerfully reflect on your understanding of and participation in the Eucharist. Going to Mass can be so much a part of our 'routine' that we can be there in body, but not fully engaged in spirit. The Mass is a ritual in which we can encounter Christ again and again in a variety of ways. Here, Jesus himself is truly and personally present. Yet, it is possible for us to hear the Scriptures being read, but not to encounter Christ there. It is possible for us to be oblivious to his presence in the Church assembled in his name. It is possible even for us to receive Holy Communion, eat his Body and drink his Blood, but still fail to recognise him and to meet with him in our prayer and meditation.

In presenting *Sharing in His Life* to you I am particularly pleased that it coincides with Pope Benedict's apostolic exhortation. The Holy Father reminds us of the call to be Eucharist – to be Christ – for the world, and movingly restates the invitation issued to us by the Second Vatican Council; not to be strangers or silent spectators at the Eucharist, but to participate consciously, actively and devoutly. My prayer, in using this resource, is that the richness of the liturgy will be opened to you, your participation in the Eucharist deepened, and your thanksgiving to God enriched.

With my blessing and prayers

+ Cormac Murphy-O'Connor

Cardinal Cormac Murphy-O'Connor
Archbishop of Westminster

Sharing in His Life is an opportunity to reflect on our celebration of the Mass. Running over six weeks, *Sharing in His Life* includes six group sessions for small groups or communities, as well as a series of daily meditations which you may wish to use on you own. Each week we will concentrate on a particular aspect of the Mass. Week 1 (Gathering), Week 2 (Word), Week 3 (Thanksgiving), Week 4 (Communion), Week 5 (Mission) and Week 6 (In Communion with Christ – Worship of the Eucharist outside Mass).

Group Sessions

These begin with an opening prayer relating to the theme of the week and drawing on the psalms. The opening prayer is followed by a scripture passage and a reflection. Following each of these there is an opportunity for the group to share their thoughts and to explore any implications for Christian living. This period of reflection and sharing can be drawn to a close using an excerpt from *Sacramentum Caritatis,* Pope Benedict XVI's exhortation on the Eucharist. The session is concluded with a series of petitions and a closing prayer.

Daily Meditations

The daily meditations on Tuesdays, Wednesdays and Thursdays will draw on the second reading from the previous Sunday. To help our preparation for the Sunday Mass the Saturday meditation will draw on the Gospel passage to be used the next day.

On Sundays, Mondays and Fridays the daily meditations will take their inspiration from the prayers of the Mass and other liturgical texts. In using these prayers and texts the writing group have been conscious of the invitation issued to priests and deacons to use these texts, as well as Scripture, as a source for their preaching.

Church Documents & Texts

A number of Church documents are referred to in the course of this booklet. You may wish to explore the following further. *Sacramentum Caritatis* (SC) is Pope Benedict XVI's recent exhortation on the Eucharist (February, 2007). *Sacramentum Caritatis* has been variously translated as 'Sacrament of Love' or 'Sacrament of Charity'. *Sacrosanctum Concilium* is the Second Vatican Council's Constitution on the Liturgy (December, 1963). Reference is also made to *Ecclesia de Eucharistia* (EE)(April, 1963), Pope John Paul II's encyclical on the relationship between the Church and the Eucharist. These documents can all be found on the Vatican website. *Celebrating the Mass* was produced by the Bishops' Conference of England and Wales in 2005.

The *Roman Missal* contains all the prayers and texts used during the Mass. It also contains the rubrics or instructions telling us how things are to be done. The *Divine Office* is a series of books containing the psalms, prayers and readings recited by priests, deacons and religious brothers and sisters on a daily basis.

From Sacrosanctum Concilium

7. Christ is always present in his Church, especially in her liturgical celebrations. He is present in the sacrifice of the Mass, not only in the person of his minister, 'the same now offering, through the ministry of priests, who formerly offered himself on the cross', but especially under the eucharistic species. By his power he is present in the sacraments, so that when a man baptises it is really Christ himself who baptises. He is present in his word, since it is he himself who speaks when the Holy Scriptures are read in the Church. He is present, lastly, when the Church prays and sings, for he promised: 'Where two or three are gathered together in my name, there am I in the midst of them' *(Matthew 18:20)*.

Opening Prayer

Leader: I was glad when they said to me,
'Let us go to the house of the lord!'

**Group: Our feet are standing within your gates,
O Jerusalem.
Jerusalem – built as a city
that is bound firmly together.**

Leader: To it the tribes go up, the tribes of the Lord,
as was decreed for Israel,
to give thanks to the name of the Lord…

**Group: Pray for the peace of Jerusalem:
'May they prosper who love you.
Peace be within your walls,
and security within your towers.'**

Leader: For the sake of my relatives and friends I will say,
'Peace be within you.'

**Group: For the sake of the house of the Lord our God,
I will seek your good.**

All: Glory be to the Father…

From Psalm 122

After a short silence, the group or an individual says:

Come then, good Shepherd, bread divine,
still show to us thy mercy sign;
oh, feed us, still keep us thine;
so we may see thy glories shine
in fields of immortality.
O thou, the wisest, mightiest, best,
our present food, our future rest,
come, make us each thy chosen guest,
co-heirs of thine, and comrades blest
with saints whose dwelling is with thee.

St. Thomas Aquinas (1225-1274)

Explore the Sunday Scriptures for the 28th Sunday in Ordinary Time Luke 17: 11 - 19

On the way to Jerusalem Jesus travelled along the border between Samaria and Galilee. As he entered one of the villages, ten lepers came to meet him. They stood some way off and called to him, 'Jesus! Master! Take pity on us.' When he saw them he said 'Go and show yourselves to the priests.' Now as they were going away they were cleansed. Finding himself cured, one of them turned back praising God at the top of his voice and threw himself at the feet of Jesus and thanked him. The man was a Samaritan. This made Jesus say, 'Were not all ten made clean? The other nine, where are they? It seems that no one has come back to give praise to God, except this foreigner.' And he said to the man, 'Stand up and go on your way. Your faith has saved you.'

Following a short period of silence you may wish to share an image, a thought, a phrase, a question that has struck you.

For Reflection

In today's gospel a group of people present themselves to Christ; a group banded together by a shared experience of suffering and the prejudices of the society in which they lived. They came to Christ in need and hope, and their hope was well founded. As they went away they were cured. One of the ten ignores Jesus' order to present himself to the priests and returns to give thanks. The seeming ingratitude of the remaining nine lepers may be disconcerting, and our reflection on this gospel, having noted the trust which all the lepers placed in Jesus, could well centre on this lack of gratitude. Again, we might readily note that it was a Samaritan, a foreigner, who came back to give thanks, taking the opportunity to remind ourselves that Christ came for all, not simply the Jews.

However, as the daily meditations for this week will focus on the gathering rites of the Mass, it may well be opportune to ask ourselves what it is that brings us to the Eucharist Sunday by Sunday. Is it a matter of habit or sense of duty that brings us, or do we come to Mass looking for something, conscious of a need or concern? Again, is what brings us a consciousness of our common baptism, a sense of our belonging to others, to a community we need to support, and that can support us?

That said, it is interesting to note that in this gospel the Samaritan, the person of faith, not only presents himself to Christ in hope and need, but also comes to him in thanks and praise to God. Faith in this gospel episode is characterised by thanksgiving and that thanksgiving stems from a joyful appreciation of all that has been given and received. The challenge one supposes is this. If our experience and understanding of faith and why we gather for the Eucharist is a matter of habit, rooted in a sense of routine, obligation and culture then it can only be a burden and our thanksgiving somewhat muted. What then is your frame of mind and heart, your 'predisposition' when you come to the Eucharist?

Share your thoughts on this reflection. How does this week's Scripture reading and reflection encourage, affirm or challenge you? What impact might this have on your daily living? To bring this period of sharing to an end the following extract may be useful.

From Sacramentum Caritatis

55. ... the Synod Fathers also discussed the personal conditions required for fruitful participation on the part of individuals. One of these is certainly the spirit of constant conversion which must mark the lives of all the faithful. Active participation in the Eucharistic liturgy can hardly be expected if one approaches it superficially, without an examination of his or her life. This inner disposition can be fostered, for example, by recollection and silence for at least a few moments before the beginning of the liturgy, by fasting and, when necessary, by sacramental confession. A heart reconciled to God makes genuine participation possible. The faithful need to be reminded that there can be no *actuosa participatio* in the sacred mysteries without an accompanying effort to participate actively in the life of the Church as a whole, including a missionary commitment to bring Christ's love into the life of society.

Leader: Aloud or in the silence of our hearts let us bring to the Father our thanks (pause)…

Leader: In sorrow let us ask the Father for forgiveness (pause)…

Leader: With confidence let us entrust to the Father our cares and concerns (pause)…

Almighty God,
help us to encourage one another to walk joyfully,
our hearts filled with wonder,
towards our encounter with the Holy Eucharist,
so that we may experience and proclaim to others
the truth of the words with which Jesus took leave of his disciples:
'Lo, I am with you always, until the end of the world'.
Amen.

Adapted from Sacramentum Caritatis, 97

Where two or three are gathered together in my name, there am I in the midst of them.

Matthew 18: 20

In this first week of *Sharing in His Life* we will be concentrating on the Opening or Introductory Rites of the Mass. Here, the Liturgy invites us to gather together to:

- know ourselves as a people made one with Christ in baptism - we are reminded of this when together with the priest we make the sign of the Cross, and say the words first said over all of us at our baptism: In the name of the Father and of the Son and of the Holy Spirit.

- acknowledge our sinfulness whilst remembering and trusting in the mercy of God - in the Penitential Rite or in the Blessing and Sprinkling with Holy Water which sometimes takes place.

- sing the praises of God - in the Gloria, an ancient hymn, which acknowledges God as King and Father, and Jesus as our Saviour.

From Celebrating the Mass

139. The purpose of the Introductory Rites is to ensure that the faithful, who come together as one, establish communion and dispose themselves to listen properly to God's word and to celebrate the Eucharist worthily.

At Mass today what did I notice as we gathered? What did I see and hear going on around me? Who did I speak to? And who spoke to me? What helped me to a sense of gathering with others in the communion of the Church? What hindered that sense of communion?

Prayer

Lord,
be the beginning and end
of all that we do and say.
Prompt our actions with your grace,
and complete them with your all-powerful help.
Grant this through Christ our Lord.
Amen.

From the Divine Office

Father in heaven, the hand of your loving kindness powerfully yet gently guides all the moments of our day.

Preoccupied with what is happening in the rest of our lives it can be difficult to turn our minds and hearts to what is present in the Mass. The Introductory Rites of the Mass are given to us to help us begin to pray. They are not intended to make us forget our concerns, but to turn to the Lord, bringing ourselves and all that concerns us into his presence. In the midst of all that is taking place in the world, the Mass is an opportunity to meet with Christ, to listen to his word of life, and to learn again to offer ourselves and all the circumstances of our lives to the glory of the Father.

Our pilgrimage through life is nourished by the Eucharist. What needs and concerns did you bring to the Eucharist on Sunday? What needs and concerns do you want to bring to the Lord today?

From Sacramentum Caritatis

2. In the sacrament of the altar, the Lord meets us, men and women created in God's image and likeness (cf. Genesis 1:27), and becomes our companion along the way. In this sacrament, the Lord truly becomes food for us, to satisfy our hunger for truth and freedom. Since only the truth can make us free (cf. John 8:32), Christ becomes for us the food of truth.

Prayer

Yesterday, the prayer below may have caught your attention. Take this opportunity to meditate on the riches it sets before us.

Father in heaven,
the hand of your loving kindness
powerfully yet gently guides all the moments of our day.
Go before us in our pilgrimage of life,
anticipate our needs and prevent our falling.
Send your Spirit to unite us in faith,
that sharing in your service,
we may rejoice in your presence.
We ask this through Christ our Lord.
Amen.

Alternative Opening Prayer for 28th Sunday of the Year

About the Opening Prayer

The Opening Prayer follows the Penitential Rite and is introduced by the priest with the words 'Let us pray'. Sometimes the priest may add a few words encouraging the assembly to pray for a particular intention. The pause which follows the priest's invitation to pray is an opportunity for everyone to offer to God his or her own prayer. At the conclusion of the silence the priest gathers together the prayers of those present, and offers petition to the Father. It is for this reason that the Opening Prayer is referred to as the Collect. It is the collecting of all the prayers, needs and intentions offered by those who have gathered.

The Second Reading for the 28th Sunday of Ordinary Time

Remember the Good News that I carry. 'Jesus Christ risen from the dead, sprung from the race of David'; it is on account of this that I have my own hardships to bear, even to being chained like a criminal - but they cannot chain up God's news. So I bear it all for the sake of those who are chosen, so that in the end they may have the salvation that is in Christ Jesus and the eternal glory that comes with it.

Here is a saying that you can rely on:

If we have died with him, then we shall live with him.
If we hold firm, then we shall reign with him.
If we disown him, then he will disown us.
We may be unfaithful, but he is always faithful,
for he cannot disown his own self.

2 Timothy 2:8-13

The Second Letter of St. Paul to Timothy is often grouped with the First Letter to Timothy and the Letter to Titus under the title of the Pastoral Epistles. Most scholars suggest that these letters were not actually written by Paul himself, but originate from the churches founded by Paul, and are written to extend the Pauline heritage into the circumstances of a later generation. Even so, the Church acknowledges these letters as inspired Scripture, the Word of God. 2 Timothy takes the form of a spiritual Last Will and Testament. Its writer urges Timothy (or the contemporary leaders of the Church) to live faithfully and to bear witness to the gospel of Jesus Christ.

In this particular passage Paul refers to the persecution and suffering he endured because of his faith. Yet he speaks of this faith as Good News. It is a source of life for him here and now, even in the midst of his difficulties. It also contains great promise for the future. The way of faith is not always an easy one to follow. Sometimes when we come to Mass we are keenly aware of the burden we bear, even, sometimes, of our failure to live faithfully which can seem too onerous a challenge. But whatever the difficulty, whatever the failures, Paul testifies 'they cannot chain up God's news.'

How do our sufferings provide us with an opportunity to share the Good News?

Prayer

The following prayer is said by the priest after the Our Father. In asking the Lord's protection this prayer can help us recognise the trust the Church places in God.

Deliver us, Lord, from every evil,
and grant us peace in our day.
In your mercy keep us free from sin
and protect us from all anxiety
as we wait in joyful hope
for the coming of our Saviour, Jesus Christ.

Roman Missal, Communion Rite, 126

I bear all for the sake of those who are chosen...

2 Timothy 2:10

Paul's faithfulness is not a private matter, something personal just between him and his God. He lives faithfully also 'for the sake of those [others] who are chosen, so that in the end they [too] may have the salvation that is in Christ Jesus and the eternal glory that comes with it'. Moreover, Paul lives faithfully in communion with those others who, like him, have already learnt to put their trust in the Good News of the mercy of God. At the beginning of Mass, in the Penitential Rite, we are invited to remember again the mercy of God and to pray for that mercy to be poured out on us and on the whole Church.

Although today's Scripture is taken from a letter addressed to Timothy, it speaks to all who are brothers and sisters in the faith. Through his knowledge and love of God, Paul finds himself caught up in that very love of God - the love of God is active in him and is poured out in the service of the world. So too for us: together, we are refreshed by the Lord's saving love, that we may be witnesses, even ministers, of his love to the world.

What burdens have you consciously carried for others? When have you been able to affirm the faith of others?

Prayer

The following words may have been used during Sunday's Penitential Rite. Pray them today and notice how they invite us to a greater awareness of what the Lord has done and will do.

Lord Jesus, you came to gather the nations into the peace of God's kingdom:
Lord, have mercy…
You come in word and sacrament to strengthen us in holiness:
Christ, have mercy…
You will come in glory with salvation for your people:
Lord, have mercy…

Roman Missal, Penitential Rite c ii

About the Penitential Rite

The Missal provides a variety of forms and texts for the Penitential Rite. Those preparing the liturgy are invited to choose the most appropriate to the season or particular occasion. The 'I Confess' form is most suitable for Lent. The second form 'Lord we have sinned against you/Lord have mercy; Lord, show us your mercy and love/And grant us your salvation' is especially suited to Ordinary Time. The third form, which has the form of a litany of praise - an example of which is given above - is likewise especially suitable for Ordinary Time and for the seasons of Easter, Advent and Christmas.

> If we have died with him, then we shall live with him. If we hold firm, then we shall reign with him. If we disown him, then he will disown us...
>
> *2 Timothy 2:11-12*

There are a lot of 'Ifs' in these few sentences. On a first reading they may seem to suggest that God's love for us depends on our behaviour. And yet, as Paul reminds us, although we can be unfaithful God cannot. Elsewhere John puts things very boldly and clearly; 'God is love' (1 John 4:8). The outpouring of love which is God's mercy is not something we have earned. It does not testify to our merits, rather it is proof of our very great need. Above all it is a testimony to how and who God is. Again, as St. John puts it very well: 'This is the love I mean: not our love for God, but God's love for us when he sent his Son to be the sacrifice that takes our sins away' (1 John 4:10). Nothing we do, or fail to do, can change the very nature of God. Even when we are consumed by fear and are failing, God is love. His love, always, seeks to win us for himself, to restore us to life and health, even from death itself.

In what particular areas of your life are you most aware of your need for the forgiveness and healing that God can give?

Prayer

The following prayer is taken from one of the prayers for the Blessing of Water which may have been used at the beginning of Mass on Sunday.

Lord,
in your mercy give us living water,
always springing up as a fountain of salvation:
free us, body and soul, from every danger,
and admit us to your presence in purity of heart.
Grant this through Christ our Lord.
Amen.

Roman Missal, The Rite of Blessing and Sprinkling of Holy Water (B)

You are a chosen race, a royal priesthood, a consecrated nation, a people set apart to sing the praises of God who called you out of the darkness into his wonderful light.

I Peter 2:9

Who celebrates the liturgy? In the Catechism we are told that the liturgy is an action of the whole Christ (Christus totus), the whole Church. It is not the work of priests and bishops alone. Rather, as we are reminded in the First Letter of Peter, all the baptised are called to 'sing the praises of God'. However, our understanding of Church extends beyond the gathered and clearly visible assembly. At the liturgy, it is the whole Church, in heaven and on earth and united with Christ its head, which celebrates (cf. Catechism of the Catholic Church, 1136-1144).

The Eucharist is a foretaste of the final or heavenly banquet, when all of us, the people of every time and age will be gathered around Christ. Put simply, the liturgy takes us beyond this current time and place. It is not just 'any' prayer and it does not 'start' when we 'start', with the ringing of a bell or the singing of a hymn. The liturgy, that unites heaven and earth, around Christ its head, is an ongoing and eternal liturgy. He is the one high priest of the true sanctuary who continually intercedes to the Father on our behalf. Here, his prayer becomes our prayer, and our prayer is caught up in his.

In the Eucharist earth and heaven meet, Christ and his kingdom is all in all, and you and I keep company with the angels, saints and peoples of every time and age. So, when next asked, who was at Mass, what will you say?

From Sacramentum Caritatis

32. The eucharistic celebration, in which we proclaim that Christ has died and risen, and will come again, is a pledge of the future glory in which our bodies too will be glorified. Celebrating the memorial of our salvation strengthens our hope in the resurrection of the body and in the possibility of meeting once again, face to face, those who have gone before us marked with the sign of faith.

Prayer

You may have heard the following preface at Mass last Sunday. Using words from the First Letter of Peter, it is a proclamation of the baptismal identity that unites us to Christ, making us sharers in his triumph over sin and death.

Father, all-powerful and ever-living God,
we do well always and everywhere to give you thanks
through Jesus Christ our Lord.
Through his cross and resurrection
he freed us from sin and death
and called us to the glory that has made us
a chosen race, a royal priesthood,
a holy nation, a people set apart.
Everywhere we proclaim your mighty works
for you have called us out of darkness
into your own wonderful light.
And so, with all the choirs of angels in heaven
we proclaim your glory
and join in their unending hymn of praise:
Holy, Holy Holy Lord...

Roman Missal, Preface of Sundays in Ordinary Time I

The Gospel for 29th Sunday in Ordinary Time

Jesus told his disciples a parable about the need to pray continually and never lose heart. 'There was a judge in a certain town' he said 'who had neither fear of God nor respect for man. In the same town there was a widow who kept on coming to him and saying, "I want justice from you against my enemy!" For a long time he refused, but at last he said to himself, "Maybe I have neither fear of God nor respect for man, but since she keeps pestering me I must give this widow her just rights, or she will persist in coming and worry me to death."'

And the Lord said, 'You notice what the unjust judge has to say? Now will not God see justice done to his chosen who cry to him day and night even when he delays to help them? I promise you, he will see justice done to them, and done speedily. But when the Son of Man comes, will he find any faith on earth?'

Luke 18:1-8

Women have an especially significant role in the gospel of St. Luke. St. Luke gives greater attention to the role of Our Lady than any of the other evangelists, except perhaps St. John. However elsewhere in his gospel too, both in the narratives and in the parables, women feature with greater frequency than in any of the other gospels. The role of women, in Luke's time, was greatly restricted, and yet in Luke's gospel it is often a woman who is set before us as a model of faithfulness.

Luke places this particular parable in the long section of his gospel which describes Jesus' journey to Jerusalem and the events of the Passion. Scholars suggest that for Luke's contemporaries the passage would have had particular significance as they came to terms with the fact that the return of the Son of Man, the Second Coming, was not going to take place as soon as the first Christians seem to have expected. They were called to be faithful not just for the short term but for the long term. Living faithfully was going to prove more challenging than they had first envisaged. Through the gospel Jesus speaks directly to their situation, even as he does, now, to ours.

Where do you find yourself in this gospel passage? Do you more closely associate yourself with the judge, or with the woman, with the disciples listening to the story, or even with Jesus himself as he offers this teaching to them?

Prayer

Come down, O love divine,
Seek thou this soul of mine,
and visit it with thine own ardour glowing;
O Comforter draw near,
within my heart appear,
and kindle it, thy holy flame bestowing.

Bianco da Siena (c.1350 - 1434)

Opening Prayer

Leader:	I bow down toward your holy temple and give thanks to your name for your steadfast love and your faithfulness;
Group:	**For you have exalted your name and your word above everything...**
Leader:	All the kings of the earth shall praise you, O Lord for they have heard the words of your mouth.
Group:	**They shall sing of the ways of the Lord, for great is the glory of the Lord.**
Leader:	For though the Lord is high, he regards the lowly; but the haughty he perceives from far away.
All:	**Glory be to the Father...**

From Psalm 138

After a short silence, the group or an individual says:

Come then, good Shepherd, bread divine,
still show to us thy mercy sign;
oh, feed us, still keep us thine;
so we may see thy glories shine
in fields of immortality.
O thou, the wisest, mightiest, best,
our present food, our future rest,
come, make us each thy chosen guest,
co-heirs of thine, and comrades blest
with saints whose dwelling is with thee.

St. Thomas Aquinas (1225-1274)

Explore the Sunday Scriptures for the 29th Sunday in Ordinary Time 2 Timothy 3:14 – 4:2

You must keep to what you have been taught and know to be true; remember who your teachers were, and how, ever since you were a child, you have known the holy Scriptures – from these you can learn the wisdom that leads to salvation through faith in Christ Jesus. All Scripture is inspired by God and can profitably be used for teaching them to be holy. This is how the man who is dedicated to God becomes fully equipped and ready for any good work.

Before God and before Christ Jesus who is to be judge of the living and the dead, I put this duty to you, in the name of his Appearing and of his kingdom: proclaim the message and, welcome or unwelcome, insist on it. Refute falsehood, correct error, call to obedience – but do all with patience and with intention of teaching.

Following a short period of silence you may wish to share an image, a thought, a phrase, a question that has struck you.

For Reflection

St. Caesarius of Arles (Bishop and theologian, 470 – 543), once posed the following question. Which to you seems the greater, the Word of God or the Body of Christ? In posing this question, St. Caesarius was really asking whether or not we afford the Word of God the dignity it deserves. Kneeling, as we do, for the Eucharistic Prayer, we physically acknowledge the importance of what is happening, as the bread and wine become the Body and Blood of Christ, but as we sit and listen to the Scriptures it's easier to be distracted, more tempting to read the newsletter. Similarly, we may more readily appreciate the reverence that surrounds the breaking of the host before the distribution of communion, than the attentiveness which the homily - or breaking open of the Word – also calls for.

The Word of God is not simply a book to be read or something to get through before we arrive at the Eucharist and Holy Communion. For us, the Word of God is Jesus who was with God and is God (John 1:1-14). In the reading of Scriptures, as in the Eucharist, we are met by Christ the Word made flesh (John 1:14).

In the Second Letter to Timothy, St. Paul reminds us, that the Scriptures will teach us how to be holy as Christ does in words and example. Here, in the Word of God, we have 'the wisdom that leads to salvation', by listening to it, we can become 'fully equipped and ready for any good work'. Quite simply, the Word of God, the Scriptures, can never be an incidental part of our Christian life. Indeed, it is in the Scriptures, in the Old and in the New Testaments, that we are told over and over of the God who is love; a God who reaches out to his people Israel and who, in Christ, reveals the depth of his love for us. Appreciating this, and truly understanding the Word to be a proclamation of love, Paul's insistence on our proclaiming the Gospel, even where it is unwelcome, is not a matter of our imposing, but the most loving thing we can do.

Share your thoughts on this reflection. How does this week's Scripture reading and reflection encourage, affirm or challenge you? What impact might this have on your daily living? To bring this period of sharing to an end the following extract may be useful.

From Sacramentum Caritatis

44. .. There is an intrinsic bond between the Word of God and the Eucharist. From listening to the Word of God, faith is born or strengthened (cf. Romans 10:17); in the Eucharist the Word made flesh gives himself to us as our spiritual food. Thus, 'from the two tables of the Word of God and the Body of Christ, the Church receives and gives to the faithful the bread of life.' Consequently it must constantly be kept in mind that the Word of God, read and proclaimed by the Church in the liturgy, leads to the Eucharist as to its own connatural end.

Leader:	Aloud or in the silence of our hearts let us bring to the Father our thanks (pause)…
Leader:	In sorrow let us ask the Father for forgiveness (pause)…
Leader:	With confidence let us entrust to the Father our cares and concerns (pause)…

Prayer

Almighty God,
help us to encourage one another to walk joyfully,
our hearts filled with wonder,
towards our encounter with the Holy Eucharist,
so that we may experience and proclaim to others
the truth of the words with which Jesus took leave of his disciples:
'Lo, I am with you always, until the end of the world'.
Amen.

Adapted from Sacramentum Caritatis, 97

You have given us your word as a light to shine upon our path…

This week we will be concentrating on the Liturgy of the Word. The Church teaches us that at Mass we are nourished spiritually at two tables: the table of God's word and the altar of Sacrifice. In the Word of God we hear afresh the divine covenant: the promises God makes to us, and the faithful life to which he calls us. In the Eucharist the new and everlasting covenant is renewed. The spoken word of God brings to mind the history of salvation; the Eucharist embodies it in the sacramental signs of the liturgy.

If we are to be nourished by God's word it is not enough for that word to be read or proclaimed. It needs to be heard, and taken to mind and heart. We need to hear the Lord speak, to prepare a space and a time for listening, not only in our liturgy, after the various readings, but in the course of the week as well. With the help of the Holy Spirit, such times of silence will help us take the word to ourselves, and to respond to the word in our prayer.

When and where in the course of the week can you take the time to prayerfully reflect on the Scriptures?

From Sacramentum Caritatis

45. …The faithful should be helped to appreciate the riches of Sacred Scripture found in the lectionary through pastoral initiatives, liturgies of the word and reading in the context of prayer (lectio divina). By praying the Psalms, the Scripture readings and the readings drawn from the great tradition which are included in the Divine Office, we can come to a deeper experience of the Christ-event and the economy of salvation, which in turn can enrich our understanding and participation in the celebration of the Eucharist.

Prayer

Lord God,
you have given us your word
as a light to shine upon our path;
grant us so to meditate on that word,
and to follow its teaching,
that we may find in it the light that shines
more and more until the perfect day.
Amen.

A prayer of St. Jerome

About the Sunday Readings

The Sunday readings are selected according to particular
patterns. Each year we read our way through one of the synoptic
gospels. This year (Year C) we read the Gospel of Luke. Last year
(Year B) we read Mark. Next year (Year A) it will be Matthew.
During Ordinary Time, which is the time of year outside of the
great liturgical seasons of Lent and Easter, Advent and Christmas,
all three of the Sunday readings, together with the psalm, explore
the themes of the season. On these Sundays of Ordinary Time
the gospel reading is simply the 'next' section from the Gospel
of that year, and the first reading is chosen because of its close
relationship to it. The second reading is taken from the other
writings of the New Testament.

Remove the blindness that cannot know you...relieve the fear that would hide us from your sight.

Very often the prayers which we use in the liturgy are a mosaic of phrases and images drawn from the various books of the Bible. The more we enter into Scripture, open the Bible, the richer our appreciation of these prayers will become. A closer look at the Opening Prayer used on Sunday, which is included today's meditation, and can be used for our private prayer, will help us to appreciate this.

• guard us under the shadow of your wings - In Psalm 91, the psalmist sings: He who dwells in the shelter of the Most High and abides in the shade of the Almighty, says to the Lord: My refuge, my stronghold, my God in whom I trust... He will conceal you with his pinions and under his wings you will find refuge.'

• the blindness that cannot know you - In chapter 9 of John's gospel we read of Jesus' healing of the man born blind, and of the spiritual blindness that keeps others from knowing Jesus.

• relieve the fear that would hide us - In Genesis chapter 3 we hear how, after their unfaithfulness, Adam and Eve, aware of their sin, become afraid of God and hid.

From Sacrosanctum Concilium

24. Sacred Scripture is of the greatest importance in the celebration of the liturgy. For it is from it that lessons are read and explained in the homily, and psalms are sung. It is from the Scriptures that the prayers, collects and hymns draw their inspiration and their force, and that actions and signs derive their meaning. Hence it is essential to promote that sweet and living love for Sacred Scripture to which the venerable tradition of the Eastern and Western rites gives testimony.

Prayer

Lord our God, Father of all,
you guard us under the shadow of your wings
and search into the depths of our hearts.
Remove the blindness that cannot know you
and relieve the fear that would hide us from your sight.
We ask this through Christ our Lord.
Amen.

Roman Missal, Opening Prayer for 29th Sunday in Ordinary Time

From the Sunday Scriptures for the 29th Sunday of Ordinary Time

You must keep to what you have been taught and know to be true; remember who your teachers were, and how, ever since you were a child, you have known the holy Scriptures - from these you can learn the wisdom that leads to salvation through faith in Christ Jesus. All Scripture is inspired by God and can profitably be used for teaching, for refuting error, for guiding people's lives and teaching them to be holy. This is how the man who is dedicated to God becomes fully equipped and ready for any good work.

Before God and before Christ Jesus who is to be judge of the living and the dead, I put this duty to you, in the name of his Appearing and of his kingdom: proclaim the message and, welcome or unwelcome, insist on it. Refute falsehood, correct error, call to obedience - but do all with patience and with the intention of teaching.

2 Timothy 3:14 - 4:2

In this letter Paul, the experienced teacher of the faith, writes to Timothy, encouraging him in the responsibilities of leadership that are now his. However, the wisdom contained in Paul's advice is not only for Timothy. It is for us too. The Word of God is a living word, alive and active (Hebrews 4:12), and the challenge for us is that of receiving the wisdom offered at a particular time, in a particular circumstance, and seeking after what it has to teach us today. In doing so we must be careful not to twist or shape the Word of God to say what we want it to say. Our task is not to dominate the word, but to listen to it as deeply as we can. Through that faithful listening, assisted by the Holy Spirit, we hear what God has spoken, a wisdom ever-ancient and ever-new.

What can I learn from this reading of Scripture today, for my life?

Prayer

Before he proclaims the gospel the priest quietly prays the words below. Today you are invited to make these words your own; praying for the grace to listen, hear and witness to the gospel as you go about your daily life.

Almighty God,
cleanse my heart and lips
that I may worthily proclaim your gospel.

Roman Missal, Ordinary of Mass, II

All Scripture is inspired by God and can profitably be used for teaching, for refuting error, for guiding people's lives and teaching them to be holy.

2 Timothy 3:16

At Mass there are a number of ways in which we show our reverence for the Word of God. After each reading we profess our faith that this is truly the living Word of God. The reader will say: 'This is the word of the Lord', and we all respond 'Thanks be to God'. Similarly as we prepare to listen to the Gospel, knowing the particular dignity of this reading we stand and sing God's praises, and we trace the sign of the Cross on our forehead, lips and heart: on our forehead that we might understand, on our heart that we might love this word, and on our lips that we might not keep this Good News to ourselves. These actions could easily be used before our personal reading of the Scriptures outside of Mass.

Where has a careful listening to the Word of God inspired the important decisions of your life?

Prayer

After proclaiming the gospel, as he kisses the Gospel Book, the priest or deacon prays the following prayer. Pray it today, asking God's forgiveness for the times his word has been ignored, but trusting in the transformation that a greater hearing will bring about.

May the words of the gospel wipe away our sins.

Roman Missal, Ordinary of Mass, 13

Proclaim the message and, welcome or unwelcome, insist on it - but do all with patience and with the intention of teaching.

2 Timothy 4:2

The word that gives us life is not given to us for ourselves alone, but as Good News to be shared far and wide; sometimes through words, but also through actions.

The world is calling for evangelisers to speak to it of a God whom the evangelists themselves should know and be familiar with as if they could see the invisible. The world calls for and expects from us simplicity of life, the spirit of prayer, charity towards all, especially towards the lowly and the poor, obedience and humility, detachment and self-sacrifice. Without this mark of holiness, our word will have difficulty in touching the heart of modern man. It risks being vain and sterile. *(Paul VI, Evangelii Nuntiandi, 76)*

We are not always perfect. But when things do go wrong, our readiness to say sorry for the things which are our fault, and to show forgiveness to others, are themselves witnesses to the life of faith. In our weaknesses, as well as our strengths, we can help others begin a journey which will lead them to a deeper knowledge and love of God.

In the face of hostility have I failed to proclaim the Good News? What, in words and actions, weakness and suffering, have others helped me to learn about the faith?

Prayer

On Sunday we prayed the following Prayer after Communion. As used here the word eucharist refers to the whole Mass, not only the sacrament of Christ's Body and Blood. With this prayer we pray to God that the gift of both word and sacrament may be fruitful for us:

Lord,
may this eucharist help us to remain faithful.
May it teach us the way to eternal life.
Grant this through Christ our Lord.
Amen.

Roman Missal, Prayer after Communion for 29th Sunday in Ordinary Time.

Even when man disobeyed you and lost your friendship you did not abandon him to the power of death, but helped all men to seek and find you.

The Old Testament speaks again and again of the unfaithfulness of God's chosen people; of leaders turning from God, and placing their trust elsewhere. In the gospels we hear how the disciples, by their words and actions, often failed to understand Jesus. In the Acts of the Apostles and the writings of Paul we see how the communities of the Church got caught up in controversy and risked losing sight of what Christ had to say.

Despite the frequent accounts of the unfaithfulness and weakness of God's people, more striking and frequent still are the passages which speak of the faithfulness of God. God is there, watching and waiting: not to catch us out, but to use these times of weakness as opportunities to do a new thing, to win us back to his way of life.

When or where have you been surprised by the saving love of God?

Prayer

Eucharistic Prayer IV is not commonly used, but the biblical imagery it draws on in recounting God's saving love is particularly moving. In conclusion to today's meditation pray this prayer of thanksgiving slowly.

Father, we acknowledge your greatness:
all your actions show your wisdom and love.
You formed man in your own likeness and set him over the whole world
to serve you, his creator, and to rule over all creatures.
Even when he disobeyed you and lost your friendship
you did not abandon him to the power of death,
but helped all men to seek and find you.
Again and again you offered a covenant to man,
and through the prophets taught him to hope for salvation.
Father, you so loved the world
that in the fullness of time you sent your only Son to be our Saviour.
He was conceived through the power of the Holy Spirit,
and born of the Virgin Mary, a man like us in all things but sin.
To the poor he proclaimed the good news of salvation,
to prisoners, freedom, and to those in sorrow, joy.
In fulfilment of your will he gave himself up to death;
but by rising from the dead, he destroyed death and restored life.
And that we might live no longer for ourselves but for him,
he sent the Holy Spirit from you, Father,
as his first gift to those who believe,
to complete his work on earth and bring us the fullness of grace.

Roman Missal, Eucharistic Prayer IV, 118

About the Sunday Gospel

Every year as we read our way through one of the gospels we can discern its original structure. This year we have listened to the Gospel of Luke. Luke divides his account of Christ's ministry into two parts, structuring it around a time of ministry in Galilee and a time of ministry in Jerusalem. He joins these sections together with the Travel Narrative, an account of Christ's journey up to Jerusalem.

In the introduction to the Lectionary the various sections or 'units' of the gospel have been listed. Noting these can be a great help to homilists and those and those involved in liturgy planning. It will help them to get a sense for the shape of the liturgy, and prepare their homilies and liturgies in sequences, rather than treating each one as entirely discrete. It will also help other members of the congregation recognise the connections between the gospels being read from Sunday to Sunday.

The gospel for the 29th Sunday in Ordinary Time comes in a section of the Travel Narrative in Luke's gospel which addresses the obstacles facing those who follow Jesus. This particular section began on the 25th Sunday with the story of the unjust steward and will end on the 31st Sunday with the story of Zacchaeus.

The Gospel for 30th Sunday in Ordinary Time

Jesus spoke the following parable to some people who prided themselves on being virtuous and despised everyone else. 'Two men went up to the Temple to pray, one a Pharisee, the other a tax collector. The Pharisee stood there and said this prayer to himself, "I thank you, God, that I am not grasping, unjust, adulterous like the rest of mankind, and particularly that I am not like this tax collector here. I fast twice a week; I pay tithes on all I get." The tax collector stood some distance away, not daring even to raise his eyes to heaven; but he beat his breast and said, "God, be merciful to me, a sinner." This man, I tell you, went home again at rights with God; the other did not. For everyone who exalts himself will be humbled, but the man who humbles himself will be exalted.'

Luke 18:9-14

Luke knows that living the life of faith is not just about the inner life. Activities such as almsgiving, fasting and prayer are integral to the life of the disciple, and characteristic of the life of the Church. But they are not ends in themselves, and less still are they something for us to boast about to God. In the parable above, the Pharisee does not even get round to boasting to God: his 'prayer' is something he addresses to himself! Moreover, we are not told what good and loving things the tax-collector did, nor the sins he committed. From the parable all we know is that in his prayer, the tax-collector freely admits to God his need for mercy and forgiveness. Indeed, Jesus does not even tell us whether or not the tax-collector knows he is going home 'at rights with God'. Nonetheless, despite the gaps, Jesus makes sure that we know and understand how God sees things.

What is comforting about the teaching of this parable? What might people find to be disturbing?

Prayer

In these words from Eucharistic Prayer IV, the Church looks to the generosity of God; not trusting in her own achievements but in the sacrifice God has given to us and the gift of his Holy Spirit which gathers us together.

Lord, look upon this sacrifice which you have given to your Church; and by your Holy Spirit, gather all who share this one bread and one cup into the one body of Christ, a living sacrifice of praise.

Roman Missal, Eucharistic Prayer IV, 123

How many Eucharistic Prayers are there?

For many years the Roman Catholic Church used just one Eucharistic Prayer, often referred to as the Roman Canon (c. fourth century). Today there are eleven Eucharistic Prayers approved for use in England and Wales. Eucharistic Prayer II is an adaptation of a prayer first known in a document thought to date from the third century. Eucharistic Prayer III was a new composition, with an especially rich intercessory section where we pray for both the living and the dead. Eucharistic Prayer IV draws on the prayer traditions of the Church in the East. In the 1980s and 90s these prayers were joined by Eucharistic Prayers for Reconciliation, for Masses with Children, and for Mass with the Deaf. More recently the Church has approved a further Eucharistic Prayer for Various Needs and Occasions which offers a series of four texts. These texts acknowledge Christ as the Compassion of God and our way to the Father, and recognise the graces the Church receives as she seeks to journey to greater unity on the way of salvation.

Opening Prayer

Leader: Make a joyful noise to the Lord,
all the earth.
Worship the Lord with gladness;
come into his presence singing.

Group: **Know that the Lord is God.**
It is he that made us, and we are his;
we are his people,
and the sheep of his pasture.

Leader: Enter his gates with thanksgiving,
and his courts with praise.
Give thanks to him,
bless his name.

Group: **For the Lord is good;**
his steadfast love endures forever,
and his faithfulness to all generations.

All: **Glory be to the Father...**

Psalm 100

After a short silence, the group or an individual says:

Come then, good Shepherd, bread divine,
still show to us thy mercy sign;
oh, feed us, still keep us thine;
so we may see thy glories shine
in fields of immortality.
O thou, the wisest, mightiest, best,
our present food, our future rest,
come, make us each thy chosen guest,
co-heirs of thine, and comrades blest
with saints whose dwelling is with thee.

St. Thomas Aquinas (1225-1274)

Explore the Sunday Scriptures for the 30th Sunday in Ordinary Time
The Responsorial Psalm: Ps 32: 2-3, 17-19. 23. R v. 7

R. This poor man called; the Lord heard him

I will bless the Lord at all times
his praise always on my lips;
in the Lord my soul shall make its boast.
The humble shall hear and be glad.

The Lord turns his face against the wicked
to destroy their remembrance from the earth.
The just call and the Lord hears
And rescues them in all their distress.

The Lord is close to the broken-hearted;
those whose spirit is crushed he will save.
The Lord ransoms the souls of his servants.
Those who hide in him shall not be condemned.

*Following a short period of silence you may wish to share an image,
a thought, a phrase, a question that has struck you.*

For Reflection

For centuries the Church has used the psalms to sing the praises of
God. They are ideal expressions of mankind's thirst and hunger for
God and of God's loving response to mankind. This psalm, said or
sung, from the 30th Sunday in Ordinary Time (Year C), is a
remarkable hymn of praise and thanksgiving to God. The very word
Eucharist used for the whole service of the Mass comes from the
Greek for thanksgiving. Mass is a sacrifice of praise and thanksgiving
in which Christ is present both as priest and victim. Our sharing in
this sacrifice, in this thanksgiving, is central to our faith.

What is it that we witness in the Eucharist? What has the Lord our
God given us in this most magnificent gift? God gave himself unto
death, a cruel and dehumanising death out of love for us. So great
was God's love, his compassion for us, that Christ was crucified, an
act re-presented during the Liturgy of the Eucharist and told of in
the Liturgy of the Word. For this we give thanks, such a gift demands
a suitable response. God shows love and compassion in this act and
this is what we are called to do in response to this gift. Our acts of
thanksgiving, our acts of Eucharist must not be confined to the walls
of the church, to the liturgy attended each Sunday but spread out
into the world. St. Ignatius talked of himself as 'God's wheat' to

become 'Christ's pure bread' through martyrdom. Though we may not end our lives as martyrs we are called to a life of spiritual witness (SC, 5). As 'God's wheat' we have the opportunity to 'feed' the world around us, to sustain people with our faithful example.

A deeper reverence for the gift of the Eucharist and the sacrifice of the Mass will naturally lead us to appreciate that a life of compassion and love must be led. As Thomas Aquinas once wrote 'God puts into his creatures, along with a kind of sheen, a reflection of God's own luminous ray'. The act of love and thanksgiving that we see in the Mass is ours to reflect in the world around us.

Now may be a good opportunity to dwell once more on Psalm 33 in the light of this reflection. How can we translate what we appreciate in the Eucharist, God's self-giving, to our daily lives? How are we able to 'feed' the world, indeed what can we 'feed' the world?

Share your thoughts on this reflection. How does this week's Scripture reading and reflection encourage, affirm or challenge you? What impact might this have on your daily living? To bring this period of sharing to an end the following extract may be useful.

From Sacramentum Caritatis

85. The first and fundamental mission that we receive from the sacred mysteries we celebrate is that of bearing witness by our lives. The wonder we experience at the gift God has made to us in Christ gives new impulse to our lives and commits us to becoming witnesses of his love... Even if the test of martyrdom is not asked of us, we know that worship pleasing to God demands that we should be inwardly prepared for it. Such worship culminates in the joyful and convincing testimony of a consistent Christian life, wherever the Lord calls us to be his witnesses.

Leader: Aloud or in the silence of our hearts let us bring to the Father our thanks (pause)...

Leader: In sorrow let us ask the Father for forgiveness (pause)...

Leader: With confidence let us entrust to the Father our cares and concerns (pause)...

Almighty God,
help us to encourage one another to walk joyfully,
our hearts filled with wonder,
towards our encounter with the Holy Eucharist,
so that we may experience and proclaim to others
the truth of the words with which Jesus took leave of his disciples:
'Lo, I am with you always, until the end of the world'.
Amen.

Adapted from Sacramentum Caritatis, 97

*a memorial proclamation of praise and thanksgiving for God's work
of salvation...*

Celebrating the Mass, 186

The celebration of the Mass progresses through various stages. We
come together as a community united with the Lord and with each
other. We listen to the Word of God proclaimed to us and in it meet
with the Lord of life. This ministry of the Word prepares us to join
with the Lord in the offering of the Sacrifice of the Mass, the new
covenant established by his blood and to receive from him the
banquet of grace which is the Eucharist. In our celebration of the
Liturgy of the Eucharist we accompany Christ in his worship of the
Father, and in the mysteries of his passion, death and resurrection, by
which he has won salvation for us. In his self-offering, we are
witnesses to love which has no parallel.

From Celebrating the Mass

174. At the Last Supper, Christ instituted the Sacrifice and Paschal
meal that make the Sacrifice of the cross present in the Church.
From the days of the Apostles the Church has celebrated that
Sacrifice by carrying out what the Lord did and handed over to
his disciples to do in his memory. The Church's Eucharist, in all its
rich variety of forms and traditions, has always retained this basic
shape: the taking of the elements of bread and wine in the
preparation of the gifts, the act of thanksgiving in the Eucharistic
Prayer, the Breaking of the Bread, the giving and sharing of the
Body and Blood of Christ in Communion.

186. The Eucharistic Prayer sums up what it means for the Church to celebrate the Eucharist. It is a memorial proclamation of praise and thanksgiving for God's work of salvation, a proclamation in which the Body and Blood of Christ are made present by the power of the Holy Spirit and the people are joined to Christ in offering his Sacrifice to the Father.

187. In the Eucharistic Prayer the mystery of Christ's saving death and resurrection is recalled; the Last Supper is recounted; the memorial Sacrifice of his Body and Blood is presented to the Father; and the Holy Spirit is invoked to sanctify the gifts and transform those who partake of them into the body of Christ, uniting the assembly and the whole Church and family of God, living and dead, into one communion of love, service, and praise to the glory of the Father.

What do I wish to give thanks to God for? How do I find myself joined to Christ in this prayer, and in my life?

Prayer

Lord Jesus Christ,
we worship you living among us
in the sacrament of your body and blood.
May we offer to our Father in heaven
a solemn pledge of undivided love.
May we offer to our brothers and sisters
a life poured out in loving service of that kingdom
where you live with the Father and the Holy Spirit,
one God, for ever and ever.
Amen.

Roman Missal, Alternative Opening Prayer for Corpus Christi

You have no need of our praise,
yet our desire to thank you is itself your gift.
Our prayer of thanksgiving adds nothing to your greatness,
but makes us grow in your grace,
through Jesus Christ our Lord.

Roman Missal, Order of Mass, Preface of Weekdays IV

The gifts of bread and wine that are brought up in procession are our gifts to God - fruit of the earth and work of human hands. Even so, as fruits of the earth they are already God's gift to us. They will be used in the Mass to symbolise the bread and wine which Jesus took, offered and shared with the disciples at the Last Supper to help the disciples begin to understand what would happen at Calvary. They will become the very Body and Blood of Christ, offered at Calvary and present now on the altar to be shared in Holy Communion. God gives first. The Church is able to celebrate and adore the mystery of Christ present in the Eucharist precisely because Christ first gave himself to her in the sacrifice of the Cross (SC, 14).

As well as the bread and wine, the Offertory Procession includes our offering of money collected to support the mission of the Church - the parish's works of faith formation and outreach to the poor and needy, as well as the up-keep of buildings and the payment of parish staff. Christ gave his all in love. In our own way, we too give in love. We give humbly from what we have certain in the knowledge that everything we bring before God 'has value in his eyes' (SC, 47).

How and where do I benefit from the gifts other people have received?
What gifts have I received that I am able to share with others?

From Sacramentum Caritatis

47. The Synod Fathers also drew attention to the presentation of the gifts. This is not to be viewed simply as a kind of 'interval' between the Liturgy of the Word and the Liturgy of the Eucharist. To do so would tend to weaken, at the least, the sense of a single rite made up of two interrelated parts. This humble and simple gesture is actually very significant: in the bread and wine that we bring to the altar, all creation is taken up by Christ the Redeemer to be transformed and presented to the Father. In this way we also bring to the altar all the pain and suffering of the world, in the certainty that everything has value in God's eyes.

Prayer

Lord God of power and might,
receive the gifts we offer
and let our service give you glory.
Grant this through Christ our Lord.
Amen.

Roman Missal, 30th Sunday in Ordinary Time, Prayer over the Gifts

The Bread and Wine

Special care is taken with regard to the quality of the bread and wine used at Mass. The bread is made from pure wheat flour, mixed only with a little water. It is made without yeast, linking it with the unleavened bread used at the Last Supper for the Passover meal. The bread should be fresh and be recently baked. The wine used at Mass is required to be natural and pure, fruit of the grape, and free from any foreign substance.

One of the earliest names for the Eucharist was the Breaking of the Bread. This sign of Breaking the Bread which, through the offering of the Sacrifice, has become the Body of Christ remains an important element of the action of the Mass. In the past a single 'loaf' was used, bringing out all the more clearly the force and importance of the sign of unity of all in the one bread, and of the sign of charity by the fact that the one bread is distributed among the brothers and sisters. Some parishes have begun once more to bake a single unleavened loaf for use at Mass, to recover this powerful sign. Where this is not possible the host used by the priest should be large enough so that, when broken, it may be shared with at least some of the congregation.

The Second Reading for the 30th Sunday of Ordinary Time

My life is already being poured away as a libation, and the time has come for me to be gone. I have fought the good fight to the end; I have run the race to the finish; I have kept the faith; all there is to come now is the crown of righteousness reserved for me, which the Lord, the righteous judge, will give to me on that Day; and not only to me but to all those who have longed for his Appearing.

The first time I had to present my defence, there was not a single witness to support me. Every one of them deserted me - may they not be held accountable for it. But the Lord stood by me and gave me power, so that through me the whole message might be proclaimed for all the pagans to hear; and so I was rescued from the lion's mouth. The Lord will rescue me from all evil attempts on me, and bring me safely to his heavenly kingdom. To him be glory for ever and ever. Amen.

2 Timothy 4:6-8.16-18

The Second Letter to Timothy was written by Paul towards the end of his life. He looks back and sees the price he has paid in responding to the Lord's love and mercy and answering the call to be an apostle. It has been a high price, much was demanded of him. At the same time, however, Paul is thankful that, with the Lord's help, he has been able to be faithful and generous in his self-giving.

At Mass, when we offer our gifts, it is hoped that what we give is at some cost, as we join our offerings to Christ's, the greatest act of giving by far. Through the Incarnation, in his becoming man, God offers himself, places himself in our hands, for our sake, to save us from sin and death. In Jesus, God continues to offer himself to us, witnessing to the Good News, seeking to lead us to share in the life of the Kingdom. How great a love has been bestowed on us, that we should not only be called children of God, but become God's children, brothers and sisters in Jesus Christ?

Have I prevented others from developing their gifts and talents, and reaching their full potential?

Prayer

Almighty and ever-living God,
strengthen our faith, hope and love.
May we do with loving hearts
what you ask of us
and come to share the life you promise.
We ask this through our Lord Jesus Christ, your Son,
who lives and reigns with you and the Holy Spirit,
one God for ever and ever.
Amen.

Roman Missal, Opening Prayer for 30th Sunday in Ordinary Time

The crown of righteousness reserved for me, which the Lord, the righteous judge, will give to me on that Day; and not only to me but to all those who have longed for his Appearing.

2 Timothy 4:8

Paul looks forward to the Second Coming of Jesus, and the judgement that will follow, confident in the Lord's righteousness. Whenever we gather to celebrate the liturgy we anticipate that Day of the Lord, for in the liturgy the Church on earth is united in worship with the Church in heaven. In this way, the Eucharist is a real foretaste of the final banquet foretold by the prophets (Isaiah 25:6-9) and described in the New Testament as 'the marriage feast of the lamb' (Revelation 19:7-9), to be celebrated in the joy of the communion of saints (SC, 31). We give expression to this in many ways in our churches and in our liturgy. For example in the statues and stained glass windows of our churches we see the saints and the angels. In our Eucharistic liturgy we always acknowledge that what we do and say and sing, we do in union with the saints and the angels, and we then sing the Sanctus, the Holy, Holy, the hymn that has its origins in the visions of Isaiah (Isaiah 6:3).

How does the Lord invite me to serve him in this life? Where am I aware of God's grace bearing fruit in my life?

Prayer

Holy, holy, holy Lord, God of power and might
heaven and earth are full of your glory.
Hosanna in the highest.
Blessed is he who comes in the name of the Lord.
Hosanna in the highest.

Roman Missal, Ordinary of the Mass, 27

> The Lord stood by me and gave me power, so that through me the whole message might be proclaimed for all the pagans to hear...
>
> *2 Timothy 4:17*

The 'whole message' of which Paul speaks is presumably the Good News entrusted to him to be shared with all peoples. That Good News can be expressed in many forms - as we see from the various writings and the ways of faithful life found in the New Testament. In the Mass the Good News finds its key expression in the Paschal Mystery, the Easter mystery of Christ's passion, death and resurrection. Our faith in this mystery is neatly professed in the Memorial Acclamations which unite the whole congregation following the words of consecration said by the priest transforming the bread and wine to the Body and Blood of Christ. Following these words, in each Eucharistic Prayer, the priest says to God the Father that we offer the sacrifice of the Mass in thanksgiving, in memory of the death and resurrection of his Son. Thanking God that this holy and perfect sacrifice can be offered in spite of ourselves, thanksgiving for this act and the gift of forgiveness is a true expression of the message of which Paul wrote.

Christ came to set us free from sin and death. What does this mean? How is this freedom reflected in your life? Where have you felt empowered by the Lord?

Prayer

The Memorial Acclamations are brief professions of faith. They can be our prayer not only at Mass, but whenever we wish to praise God for the salvation won for us in Christ.

1. *Christ has died,*
   Christ is risen,
   Christ will come again.

2. *Dying you destroyed our death,*
   rising you restored our life.
   Lord Jesus, come in glory.

3. *When we eat this bread and drink this cup,*
   we proclaim your death, Lord Jesus,
   until you come in glory.

4. *Lord, by your cross and resurrection*
   you have set us free.
   You are the Saviour of the world.

Roman Missal, Memorial Acclamations

Father, all-powerful and ever-living God,
we do well always and everywhere to give you thanks.
When your children sinned
and wandered far from your friendship,
you reunited them with yourself
through the blood of your Son
and the power of the Holy Spirit.
You gather them into your Church
to be one as you, Father, are one
with your Son and the Holy Spirit.
You call them to be your people
to praise your wisdom in all your works.
You make them the body of Christ
and the dwelling place of the Holy Spirit.
In our joy we sing to your glory
with all the choirs of angels:
Holy…

Roman Missal, Order of Mass, Preface of Sundays in Ordinary Time VIII

In this prayer we give thanks for what God has done for all his children. Some of this family of God we know, countless others we do not, but for all and with all we give thanks to God.

Sometimes, there is a tension between our need to pray as individuals and our call to pray as a community. At Mass, we pray principally as a community. However, this does not mean that the prayer is impersonal. On the contrary the hope is that each and every person present is able to join themselves with the prayer of the community in an intensely personal way.

What times in the day and in the week do you find best for your own private prayer? What joy do you find when praying with others?

From Sacramentum Caritatis

76. Wherever communion with God, which is communion with the Father, with the Son and with the Holy Spirit, is destroyed, the root and source of our communion with one another is destroyed. And wherever we do not live communion among ourselves, communion with the Triune God is not alive and true either.

Prayer

Use the Preface above for your private prayer today, feel free to change the pronouns from 'them' to 'us', or even to 'me'. What is not permitted with our liturgical prayer is perfectly proper in private as we explore the meaning of these great prayers for ourselves.

About the Preface

The Preface is the first part of a Eucharistic Prayer. It comes immediately after an introductory dialogue between the priest and the congregation in which the priest encourages the faithful to give thanks. 'Let us give thanks to the Lord', says the priest, to which the people reply, 'It is right to give him thanks and praise.' They agree that this is a proper thing to do, and the priest proceeds to thank God in the words of the preface.

The Prefaces are poetic texts, rich in their theological insights into the saving actions of God. Some Prefaces are integral to a particular Eucharistic Prayer and can only be used with that Prayer, for example the preface to Eucharistic Prayer IV. More commonly the Prefaces can be used with any Prayer that does not have its own integral preface, e.g. Eucharistic Prayers I, II, and III.

The Gospel for 31st Sunday of Ordinary Time

Jesus entered Jericho and was going through the town when a man whose name was Zacchaeus made his appearance; he was one of the senior tax collectors and a wealthy man. He was anxious to see what kind of man Jesus was, but he was too short and could not see him for the crowd; so he ran ahead and climbed a sycamore tree to catch a glimpse of Jesus who was to pass that way. When Jesus reached the spot he looked up and spoke to him: 'Zacchaeus, come down. Hurry, because I must stay at your house today.' And he hurried down and welcomed him joyfully. They all complained when they saw what was happening. 'He has gone to stay at a sinner's house,' they said. But Zacchaeus stood his ground and said to the Lord, 'Look, sir, I am going to give half my property to the poor, and if I have cheated anybody I will pay him back four times the amount.' And Jesus said to him, 'Today salvation has come to this house, because this man too is a son of Abraham; for the Son of Man has come to seek out and save what was lost.'

Luke 19:1-10

Tomorrow's gospel reading brings to a close the section of Luke's gospel which describes Jesus' journey to Jerusalem. In it we hear of how Jesus continues to win people for the Kingdom. Zacchaeus was a tax collector, he was a collaborator with the Romans and he was a sinner. All of this meant he was shunned and despised by the people he met. What people thought of Zacchaeus was not important to Jesus. He takes the initiative and invites himself into the home of Zacchaeus. He makes himself vulnerable, runs the risk of making himself ritually impure - and brings about a conversion of heart and life. What was lost is now found. The Son of Man shows himself to be a shepherd to the whole flock.

During the Mass we petition God the Father, to 'not consider what we truly deserve, but [to] grant us forgiveness'. As Christ did with Zacchaeus, forgiving him for all his wrongs and converting his mind and heart to a life in God, so Christ does for us. Christ welcomes us with open arms, no matter who we are or what we've done.

How does your parish show that it is a welcoming community? Are there still people who might not feel welcome? How do you play your own part in this work of making others welcome?

Prayer

May God bless me with every good gift from on high.
May he keep me pure and holy in his sight at all times.
May he bestow the riches of his grace upon me,
bring me the good news of salvation,
and always fill me with love for all men.
I ask this through Christ our Lord.
Amen.

Adapted from the Roman Missal, Prayers over the People, 20

Opening Prayer

Leader: Bless the Lord, O my soul.
O Lord my God, you are very great…

Group: **From your lofty abode you water the mountains;
the earth is satisfied
with the fruit of your work.**

Leader: You cause the grass to grow for the cattle,
and plants for people to use,

Group: **to bring forth food from the earth,
and wine to gladden the human heart,**

Leader: oil to make the face shine,
and bread to strengthen the human heart.

All: **Glory be to the Father…**

From Psalm 104

After a short silence, the group or an individual says:

Come then, good Shepherd, bread divine,
still show to us thy mercy sign;
oh, feed us, still keep us thine;
so we may see thy glories shine
in fields of immortality.
O thou, the wisest, mightiest, best,
our present food, our future rest,
come, make us each thy chosen guest,
co-heirs of thine, and comrades blest
with saints whose dwelling is with thee.

St. Thomas Aquinas (1225-1274)

We pray continually that our God will make you worthy of his call and by his power fulfil all your desires for goodness and complete all that you have been doing through faith; because in this way the name of our Lord Jesus Christ will be glorified in you and you in him, by the grace of our God and the Lord Jesus Christ.

To turn now, brothers, to the coming of our Lord Jesus Christ and how we shall all be gathered round him: please do not get excited too soon or alarmed by any prediction or rumour or any letter claiming to come from us, implying that the Day of the Lord has already arrived.

Following a short period of silence you may wish to share an image, a thought, a phrase, a question that has struck you.

For Reflection

Ours is a generous God, one whose glory radiates out, a glory that we are called to reflect to the world around us. We may often feel that we are failing to reflect God's glory and majesty, that our weaknesses denote unworthiness, but even a cracked mirror reflects light. As we look around us at Mass, or even in our workplace or local community we see people capable of 'shining' for others, capable of reflecting God's holy light.

In the passage above St. Paul prays that the Thessalonians be made worthy of God's call. In his letters St. Paul gives plenty of practical advice as to the living out of the 'holy' life, but throughout, as in this particular passage, there is an explicit acknowledgement that it is only through God's power and generosity that our holy living, our 'desires for goodness', our being reconciled to the Father, will be fulfilled. Every time we gather for the Eucharist we proclaim our trust in the transforming power of the Holy Spirit. We believe that bread and wine is changed into the Body and Blood of Christ and then, before feasting on that Body and Blood, we pray these words, 'Lord, I am not worthy to receive you, but only say the word and I shall be healed'.

In the Gospel for the 31st Sunday of Ordinary Time we hear how an encounter with Christ transforms the life of Zacchaeus, a senior tax collector, a wealthy man, a sinner. 'Look, sir,' says Zacchaeus to Christ, 'I am going to give half my property to the poor, and if I have cheated anybody I will pay him back four times the amount' (Luke 19: 8).

If we truly believe in the transforming power of the Holy Spirit, in a generous God, who has and will give us all that attains to holiness, our basic frame of mind or predisposition must be one of hope and trust. In God, in Christ, in the power of the Holy Spirit, everything is possible. In the Apostolic Exhortation, *Sacramentum Caritatis*, Pope Benedict calls us to a greater appreciation of the transforming power of God's Holy Spirit, reminding us that it is through the outpouring of the Holy Spirit – 'Christ's first gift to those who believe' – that the apostles were able to undertake their mission and that Christ 'continues to be present and active in his Church, starting with her vital centre which is the Eucharist' (SC, 12).

Share your thoughts on this reflection. How does this week's Scripture reading and reflection encourage, affirm or challenge you? What impact might this have on your daily living? To bring this period of sharing to an end the following extract may be useful.

From Sacramentum Caritatis

13. The spiritual life of the faithful can benefit greatly from a better appreciation of the richness of the anaphora (the Eucharistic Prayer): along with the words spoken by Christ at the Last Supper, it contains the epiclesis, the petition to the Father to send down the gift of the Spirit so that the bread and the wine will become the body and blood of Jesus Christ and that 'the community as a whole will become ever more the body of Christ'. The Spirit invoked by the celebrant upon the gifts of bread and wine placed on the altar is the same Spirit who gathers the faithful 'into one body' and makes of them a spiritual offering pleasing to the Father.

Leader: Aloud or in the silence of our hearts let us bring to the Father our thanks (pause)…

Leader: In sorrow let us ask the Father for forgiveness (pause)…

Leader: With confidence let us entrust to the Father our cares and concerns (pause)…

Prayer

Almighty God,
help us to encourage one another to walk joyfully,
our hearts filled with wonder,
towards our encounter with the Holy Eucharist,
so that we may experience and proclaim to others
the truth of the words with which Jesus took leave of his disciples:
'Lo, I am with you always, until the end of the world'.
Amen.

Adapted from Sacramentum Caritatis, 97

as a sign that even now we share in your life

In the celebration of the Mass, Christ is present to us in a variety of ways: in the people who have gathered in his name, in the ministry of the priest, in the Word of God proclaimed, and in the offering of the Sacrifice. In Holy Communion, Christ gives himself to us in a yet more tangible way, his Body and Blood as food and drink.

Receiving the Body and Blood of Christ is not something we should do lightly. In *Sacramentum Caritatis* Pope Benedict states that 'care must be taken lest they conclude that the mere fact of their being present in church during the liturgy gives them a right or even an obligation to approach the table of the Eucharist' (SC, 55). In preparation for receiving Communion the question set before us by the liturgy is do we live in communion with one another? Have we, as we pray in the Our Father, really forgiven those who 'trespass against us'? Again, when we offer the sign of peace is it a true reflection of our feelings and thoughts towards those around us or is it a mere reflex action? Moreover, can the peace which we speak of in the liturgy be found in our daily relationships?

Are we reconciled with each other? Are we reconciled to God?

From Celebrating the Mass

200. The eating and drinking together of the Lord's Body and Blood in a Paschal meal is the culmination of the Eucharist. The assembly is made ready to share in this banquet by a series of rites that lead from the Eucharistic Prayer directly to the Communion. The themes underlying these rites are the mutual love and reconciliation that are both the condition and the fruit of worthy communion and the unity of the many in the one.

Prayer

Lord Jesus Christ,
you give us your body and blood in the eucharist
as a sign that even now we share your life.
May we come to possess it completely in the kingdom
where you live for ever and ever
Amen.

The Roman Missal, Prayer after Communion for Corpus Christi

About the Communion Rite

The Communion Rite is relatively simple in its structure - a time of preparation, a time of reception, and a time for prayer following reception. It begins with our standing and praying the Lord's Prayer together. It continues with the prayer 'Deliver us, Lord, from every evil...', the acclamation 'For the kingdom, the power and the glory...', and the Prayer for Peace. It includes the exchange of the sign of peace between the members of the community gathered in prayerful anticipation. It continues with the rite of Breaking of Bread, with its song 'Lamb of God...', and the invitation to Communion. It reaches its high point as the faithful come forward to receive first the Body of the Lord, the Bread of Life, and then to receive the Blood of Christ, the Cup of Salvation. There is encouragement for this reception of Holy Communion to be accompanied by song, deepening and commenting on the sacred action. Once all have received there is to be a time of silent prayer, during which the Church contemplates and gives thanks for the mystery it shares in. Then, we come to the Prayer after Communion, marking the conclusion of the Communion Rite.

Lifted high on the cross,
Christ gave his life for us,
so much did he love us.
From his wounded side flowed blood and water,
the fountain of sacramental life in the Church.
To his open heart the Saviour invites all men,
to draw water in joy from the springs of salvation.

Roman Missal, Preface of the Sacred Heart

In the Lord's Prayer the Church, the Body of Christ, joins with Jesus, its head, in the worship of God the Father. Jesus, God made flesh, helps us to make his love of the Father our own. We join with the Son in the worship of God in glory. We honour his name, we pray for the coming of his Kingdom, the fulfilment of his will. Faithful love of the Father comes to expression in our prayer.

Jesus was God from before all time. But in time, at a particular time in our history, God the Son took to himself our human nature and became one like us in all but sin. He knows the limitations of every human being. He knows the way that sin marks the lives of individuals and society. He knows the power of temptation, and how difficult human beings find it to resist. But in his human nature he knows that the 'answer' to our neediness is the love and the power of God. As one of us, Jesus teaches us to turn to the Father in prayer, acknowledging our neediness, our weaknesses and our failures.

What is God's will for you this day? Where in the life of the world and Church can you see signs of the nearness of the kingdom of God?

From Sacramentum Caritatis

71. The Eucharist…makes possible, day by day, the progressive transfiguration of all those called by grace to reflect the image of the Son of God (cf. Romans 8:29). There is nothing authentically human – our thoughts and affections, our words and deeds – that does not find in the sacrament of the Eucharist the form it needs to be lived to the full. Here we can see the full human import of the radical newness brought by Christ in the Eucharist: the worship of God in our lives cannot be relegated to something private and individual, but tends by its nature to permeate every aspect of our existence. Worship pleasing to God thus becomes a new way of living our whole life, each particular moment of which is lifted up, since it is lived as part of a relationship with Christ and as an offering to God. The glory of God is the living man (cf. I Corinthians 10:31). And the life of man is the vision of God.

Prayer

Our Father, who art in heaven,
hallowed be thy name.
Thy kingdom come.
Thy will be done on earth, as it is in heaven.
Give us this day our daily bread,
and forgive us our trespasses,
as we forgive those who trespass against us,
and lead us not into temptation,
but deliver us from evil.
Amen.

The Lord's Prayer

The gospels contain two versions of the Lord's Prayer (Luke 11:2-4, Matthew 6:9-13). It is the longer version of the prayer, given in Matthew's gospel, that is used in the liturgy. The doxology, 'Thy Kingdom come' which Catholics pray as a separate prayer and some other churches include in the Lord's Prayer was probably a later addition. It occurs in a 1st Century liturgical document, probably from Syria, called the Didache, and in some later manuscripts of the gospels.

The prayer is traditionally associated with the Eucharist. It was taught to those preparing for baptism so that they could pray it publicly for the first time at the Mass following their baptism. This is a practice re-introduced by the RCIA for those adults preparing for baptism.

The Second Reading for the 31st Sunday of Ordinary Time

We pray continually that our God will make you worthy of his call, and by his power fulfil all your desires for goodness and complete all that you have been doing through faith; because in this way the name of our Lord Jesus Christ will be glorified in you and you in him, by the grace of our God and the Lord Jesus Christ.

To turn now, brothers, to the coming of our Lord Jesus Christ and how we shall all be gathered round him: please do not get excited too soon or alarmed by any prediction or rumour or any letter claiming to come from us, implying that the Day of the Lord has already arrived.

2 Thessalonians 1:11 - 2:2

Who is worthy to come before the Lord? Ever? At Mass, as we prepare for Holy Communion we acknowledge what we lack but more importantly we remember God's glory and generosity. In the Prayer for Peace we are called to surrender to God's will, we are told that all we depend on is a gift from God. The peace given to the apostles is one such gift. We only need 'say the word and we shall be healed'. Our trust is not in what we deserve but in his gift.

Where in my life do I draw on the peace of Christ? What witness to peace do or can I give to those around me?

Prayer

Lord Jesus Christ, you said to your apostles:
I leave you peace, my peace I give you.
Look not on our sins, but on the faith of your Church,
and grant us the peace and unity of your kingdom.

Roman Missal, Ordinary of the Mass, 127

Turn now, brothers, to the coming of our Lord Jesus Christ...

2 Thessalonians 2:1

In Holy Communion Christ comes to us in the form of food and drink, under the signs of bread and wine. And yet it is not simply under the sign of bread and wine, but bread broken, wine poured out. The very symbols of the liturgy bear witness to what Christ incurred on our behalf. The Lord of all is with us as the servant of all. In Paul's letter to the Philippians we read: 'And being found in human form, he humbled himself and became obedient unto death, even death on a cross' (Philippians 2:6-8).

In Holy Communion, the humility of the Lord is again made evident: a humility which he takes upon himself in order to offer us loving service. We are a people who hunger and thirst for life. He is our God who gives himself to us so that our hunger can be satisfied and our thirst quenched.

In what particular ways has the Lord served you, during your life?

Prayer

The Lamb of God is a litany intended to be sung during the Breaking of the Bread, the action which prepares the consecrated bread for the communion of the faithful.

The word Lamb, when applied to Jesus, reminds us of the sacrifice he made of his life and which replaced the need for any other.

Lamb of God, you take away the sins of the world: have mercy on us.
Lamb of God, you take away the sins of the world: have mercy on us.
Lamb of God, you take away the sins of the world: grant us peace.

Roman Missal, Ordinary of Mass, 131

We shall all be gathered round him...

2 Thessalonians 2:1

Asked to greet a monarch or head of state most of us would be concerned to get things right; to know what to say and do. At communion we come into the presence of Christ to receive him in Holy Communion. How much more attention should we give to our words and actions? Indeed the procession, of which we are a part, is not a queue, much as we queue for the bus. It is supposed to 'express the humble patience of the poor moving forward to be fed, the alert expectancy of God's people sharing the Paschal meal in readiness for their journey, the joyful confidence of God's people on the march toward the promised land' (*Celebrating the Mass*, 210).

How might your reception of Communion be more prayerful? How might your gestures when receiving Communion more readily express that being at one with others which our receiving Holy Communion proclaims?

Prayer

The words exchanged between ministers and communicants at the time of Communion are so simple, and the exchange so easily made, that their profundity as a shared confession of faith can easily be overlooked. Today, we have the opportunity to dwell on this dialogue – our final act of preparation before receiving Christ himself – and the faith they convey.

The Body of Christ. Amen
The Blood of Christ. Amen

Roman Missal, Order of Mass, 136, 137

Lord,
you give us new hope in this eucharist.
May the power of your love
continue its saving work among us
and bring us to the joy you promise.

Roman Missal, Prayer after Communion for 31st Sunday in Ordinary Time

The pace of life has quickened over the last century. Too few people feel able to put aside time for themselves in the midst of the barrage of information, phone calls and demands on their time. In this turmoil, this constant, insistent pace of life, there are moments for prayer. Small acts of sacrifice, self-denial, caring and love can be offered up to God.

While we have these opportunities during daily life, time set aside for prayer, meditation and silence is very precious. Immediately after the reception of Christ's Body and Blood in the Eucharist, there is an ideal time for contemplation and reflection either in silence or in song (SC, 50). Fed by Christ we have the opportunity to give thanks personally but alongside the others at Mass. Together with the Prayer after Communion this time after communion is a moment of peace in a busy world, five precious minutes that might be profitably used to put the week into perspective.

Where do you feel particular need for the strength and healing of God? Where are there opportunities for you to share with others the graces you receive in Holy Communion?

From Sacramentum Caritatis

77. Today there is a need to rediscover that Jesus Christ is not just a private conviction or an abstract idea, but a real person, whose becoming part of human history is capable of renewing the life of every man and woman…It is significant that St. Paul, in the passage of the Letter to the Romans where he invites his hearers to offer the new spiritual worship, also speaks of the need for a change in their way of living and thinking: 'Do not be conformed to this world but be transformed by the renewal of your mind, that you may prove what is the will of God, what is good and acceptable and perfect' (Romans 12:2). In this way the Apostle of the Gentiles emphasises the link between true spiritual worship and the need for a new way of understanding and living one's life. An integral part of the eucharistic form of the Christian life is a new way of thinking, 'so that we may no longer be children tossed to and fro and carried about with every wind of doctrine' (Ephesians 4:14).

Prayer

This simple prayer is given to ministers to pray during the cleansing of the vessels after communion. It is a prayer that all might say, asking for their communion to be fruitful in them.

Lord, may I receive these gifts in purity of heart.
May they bring me healing and strength, now and for ever.

Roman Missal, Order of Mass, 138.

The Gospel for 32nd Sunday in Ordinary Time

Some Sadducees - those who say that there is no resurrection - approached Jesus and they put this question to him, 'Master, we have it from Moses in writing, that if a man's married brother dies childless, the man must marry the widow to raise up children for his brother. Well, then, there were seven brothers. The first, having married a wife, died childless. The second and then the third married the widow. And the same with all seven, they died leaving no children. Finally the woman herself died. Now, at the resurrection, to which of them will she be wife since she had been married to all seven?' Jesus replied, 'The children of this world take wives and husbands, but those who are judged worthy of a place in the other world and in the resurrection from the dead do not marry because they can no longer die, for they are the same as the angels, and being children of the resurrection they are sons of God. And Moses himself implies that the dead rise again, in the passage about the bush where he calls the Lord the God of Abraham, the God of Isaac and the God of Jacob. Now he is God, not of the dead, but of the living; for to him all men are in fact alive.'

Luke 20: 27-38

Given the profound mystery that is God and God's love for the world, it is scarcely surprising that throughout the ages people have argued about faith and religion. Sometimes those arguments witness to how important faith is. Sometimes, sadly, the arguments have relatively little to do with faith and God: they have simply become ways for different groups of people to get at each other.

Perhaps the Sadducees approach Jesus looking for his help so that they might understand the truth better. But perhaps they are simply trying to trick him, to catch him out. But see who comes out of the confrontation looking best!

The Sadducees end up, deliberately or not, trivialising the mystery of salvation. Jesus calls them, and us, to deepen our understanding, and to open our hearts and minds to receive the fullness of what God offers us - life everlasting, life lived to the full.

How do I understand the promise of eternal life?

Prayer

All-powerful God,
have mercy upon our brothers and sisters
who have gone before us in faith;
may this Eucharist be for us the way to salvation
and for them the means of forgiveness.

> *Roman Missal, Prayer after Communion at Mass for all the Dead (E)*

The Prayer after Communion.

The Prayer after Communion brings the Communion Rite to a conclusion. It acknowledges and expresses gratitude for the gift we receive in Holy Communion and it asks that the gift may be fruitful in us. It is followed by the notices and any other concluding rites, including the final Blessing and Dismissal.

Week Five Group Session (Mission)

Opening Prayer

Leader: O sing to the Lord a new song;
sing to the Lord, all the earth.

Group: **Sing to the Lord, bless his name;
tell of his salvation from day to day.**

Leader: Declare his glory among the nations,
his marvellous works among all the peoples.

Group: **For great is the Lord,
and greatly to be praised;**

All: **Glory be to the Father...**

From Psalm 96

After a short silence, the group or an individual says:

Come then, good Shepherd, bread divine,
still show to us thy mercy sign;
oh, feed us, still keep us thine;
so we may see thy glories shine
in fields of immortality.
O thou, the wisest, mightiest, best,
our present food, our future rest,
come, make us each thy chosen guest,
co-heirs of thine, and comrades blest
with saints whose dwelling is with thee.

St. Thomas Aquinas (1225-1274)

Explore the Sunday Scriptures for the 32nd Sunday in Ordinary Time 2 Thessalonians 2: 16 – 3: 5

May our Lord Jesus Christ himself, and God our Father who has given us his love and, through his grace, such inexhaustible comfort and such sure hope, comfort you and strengthen you in everything good that you do or say.

Finally, brothers, pray for us; pray that the Lord's message may spread quickly, and be received with honour as it was among you; and pray that we may be preserved from the interference of bigoted and evil people, for faith is not given to everyone. But the Lord is faithful, and he will give you strength and guard you from the evil one, and we, in the Lord have every confidence that you are doing and will go on doing all that we tell you. May the Lord turn your hearts towards the love of God and the fortitude of Christ.

Following a short period of silence you may wish to share an image, a thought, a phrase, a question that has struck you.

For Reflection

Just as St. Paul prayed for the small gathering of early Christians living in Thessalonica (now, the northern Greek city of Thessaloniki) who faced their share of challenges, our celebration of the Sunday liturgy concludes with a blessing - asking our Heavenly Father to strengthen us in everything good that we do and say. While some may feel this final blessing concludes their Sunday 'obligation' and enables them 'to get on with their day,' the rite of dismissal is actually more akin to 'a launch' or a starting point than a closing. Like the apostles at the Last Supper, we, who have celebrated the Eucharist, are commissioned for eucharistic living. What does that mean?

Week Five Group Session (Mission)

In the Eucharist we encounter Christ. In the Liturgy of the Word, Christ gives us concrete examples of how to imitate him. In the Creed we recount our belief, renewing our baptismal promises and commitment to Christ. In our Eucharistic Prayer, we are given an opportunity to join our sacrifices of the previous week with Christ's - the Perfect Sacrifice. In receiving his Body and Blood we are nourished, becoming 'sharers in the divine life in an ever more adult and conscious way' (SC, 70). If we have really engaged with this encounter with Christ – the Christ who has suffered for us – if we have really understood what it is we have celebrated, then every aspect of our lives, everything we do, must and will be transfigured (SC,71). It is then that we will live 'eucharistically'; the whole of our lives – as with the Mass – will be an act of thanksgiving to God. And what is more, we will come to acknowledge our dependence upon the Eucharist, the life-giving encounter with Christ.

Not unlike the early Christians, we are continually faced with challenges in our now largely secular world. We are sharing in Christ's life and living eucharistically when we:

- stand firm in the face of assaults on our faith – just as Christ did in his final days;

- seek his strength and guidance through prayer – just as Christ prayed on many occasions;

- share in the burdens of others – just as Christ did in the course of his ministry and ultimately through his death on the Cross;

- strive to live and to proclaim the Good News – the message of the Risen Christ in the course of daily living, in our homes and places of work.

Our task, therefore, is to turn our minds and hearts again and yet again to Christ, to marvel at the mystery so that we become like the apostles at the Last Supper and those with whom Christ met on the way to Emmaus. They were so moved that they 'felt the need to share with their brothers and sisters the joy of meeting the Lord' (Luke 24:33-35). Maybe we need to consider what would help us to recover their sense of excitement and purpose?

Share your thoughts on this reflection. How does this week's Scripture reading and reflection encourage, affirm or challenge you? What impact might this have on your daily living? To bring this period of sharing to an end the following extract may be useful.

From Sacramentum Caritatis

84. There is nothing more beautiful than to know him and to speak to others of our friendship with him. These words are all the more significant if we think of the mystery of the Eucharist. The love that we celebrate in the sacrament is not something we can keep to ourselves. By its very nature it demands to be shared with all. What the world needs is God's love; it needs to encounter Christ and to believe in him. The Eucharist is thus the source and summit not only of the Church's life but also of her mission: 'an authentically Eucharistic Church is a missionary Church. We too must be able to tell our brothers and sisters with conviction: 'That which we have seen and heard we proclaim also to you, so that you may have fellowship with us.' (1 John 1:3) Truly, nothing is more beautiful than to know Christ and to make him known to others.

Leader: Aloud or in the silence of our hearts let us bring to the Father our thanks (pause)...

Leader: In sorrow let us ask the Father for forgiveness (pause)...

Leader: With confidence let us entrust to the Father our cares and concerns (pause)...

Almighty God,
help us to encourage one another to walk joyfully,
our hearts filled with wonder,
towards our encounter with the Holy Eucharist,
so that we may experience and proclaim to others
the truth of the words with which Jesus took leave of his disciples:
'Lo, I am with you always, until the end of the world'.
Amen.

Adapted from Sacramentum Caritatis, 97

Go in peace to love and serve the Lord.

During this week our liturgical focus is on the Concluding Rites of the Mass the purpose of which is to 'send the people forth to put into effect in their daily lives the Paschal Mystery and the unity in Christ which they have celebrated' and to give them ' a sense of abiding mission, which calls them to witness to Christ in the world and to bring the Gospel to the poor' (Celebrating the Mass, 217).

Here, it is interesting to note that 'Mass', our usual word for the whole celebration of the Eucharist, is derived from one of the Latin words in the traditional dismissal: Ite, missa est. In *Sacramentum Caritatis*, Pope Benedict XVI explains 'that in antiquity, missa simply meant "dismissal".' The Holy Father goes on to point out that the word missa or dismissal has taken on a deeper meaning in Christian usage, implying 'mission'. Thus in the final words of the Mass we are commanded to go out on mission to the world (SC, 51).

Each one of us is strengthened by the gift of Christ received in the Eucharist, however, with this spiritual nourishment comes a task – to live our daily lives in Christ and to imitate his example. We are given this task of developing a eucharistic spirit every Sunday, the day on which we traditionally set aside our daily concerns and habits in favour of rest and relaxation. In doing so, this day presents us with freedom not only to contemplate the Eucharist vis-à-vis our daily lives through prayer and Scripture study but also to practise works of charity - that enable us to bring into people's lives the love of Christ that we receive through the Eucharist.

As we each begin to contemplate our own mission plans, we may wish to refer to John Paul II's Apostolic Letter *Dies Domini* for further insights and specific suggestions to help us rediscover the full meaning of Sunday so that by our choices we can begin to make it truly the Lord's Day (DD, 45, 52, 72).

Take a moment to reflect on your Sunday routine. In addition to Mass how else, in your choice of activities, do you reflect the uniqueness of this day?

From Dies Domini

52. Sharing in the Eucharist is the heart of Sunday, but the duty to keep Sunday holy cannot be reduced to this. In fact, the Lord's Day is lived well if it is marked from beginning to end by grateful and active remembrance of God's saving work. This commits each of Christ's disciples to shape the other moments of the day — those outside the liturgical context: family life, social relationships, and moments of relaxation — in such a way that the peace and joy of the Risen Lord will emerge in the ordinary events of life.

Prayer

Our prayer today is the final blessing from Mass. Notice the profound things which priest and people say to each other. Give thanks for your being joined with the Lord, enriched by his blessing and being sent to share in his saving work.

The Lord be with you.
And also with you.
May almighty God bless you,
the Father, and the Son, and the Holy Spirit.
Amen.
Go in peace to love and serve the Lord.
Thanks be to God.

Roman Missal, The Order of Mass, 142, 143

Give us freedom of spirit and health in mind and body to do your work on earth.

Roman Missal, Opening Prayer for 32nd Sunday in Ordinary Time

At Mass, we receive Christ himself. And he gives himself to us not just to be with us - for he is with us in so many ways: in the gathering of the Church, in the word proclaimed, in the priest and in the offering of the Sacrifice of Praise. He gives himself to us in the form of food and drink, to unite us more deeply in communion with him, and also to build us up, nourish us, for the mission entrusted to us.

In order to help us develop our missionary character, Pope John Paul II in *Mane nobiscum Domine* (Stay with us, Lord) set forth its fundamental elements:

* a loving heart that is constantly giving thanks to God- our Creator for all that we have and are – in other words a 'Eucharistic' attitude (MND, 26);

* a mind that actively promotes communion, peace and solidarity throughout our troubled world (MND, 27);

* hands willing to serve those in greatest need, thereby committed to building a more just and fraternal society (MND, 28).

At a time when self-sufficiency has become an ideal and time has become a precious commodity, it is often quite easy to forget the needs of others and even the centrality of Christ's sacrifice in our day-to-day living. During the celebration of the Eucharist, our minds and hearts are turned towards God through our senses – singing hymns, seeing the tabernacle, and hearing the Word of God – to mention but a few. Perhaps the occasional touch of a small crucifix tucked away in a pocket might help us to continue to fix our gaze on Christ and to call to mind his love and our life in him. Perhaps a brief moment to recall Christ's sacrifice on our behalf will help us to make choices that are in keeping with his gospel message.

How can we begin to live a way of thanksgiving, solidarity and service? How, through his self-gift, does Christ help us in our earthly work?

From Celebrating the Mass

16. Active participation in the Eucharist is a transforming experience. In our prayers, and that of the whole Church, we seek the transformation not only of the bread and wine into the Body and Blood of Christ, but that the same Spirit transforms us also into the Body of Christ. But it does not end here...

17. Authentic Catholic spirituality is centred on communal celebration of the Paschal Mystery of Jesus Christ so that we may go out into the world to live that mystery, refreshed and restored as agents of God's love. The Eucharist must feed those who celebrate: for their work in the healing of relationships, in the promotion of peace and justice, and in the proclamation of the Good News.

Prayer

Lord,
we thank you for the nourishment you give us
through your holy gift.
Pour out your Spirit upon us
and in the strength of this food from heaven
keep us single-minded in your service.
We ask this through Jesus the Lord.
Amen.

Roman Missal, Closing Prayer for 32nd Sunday in Ordinary Time

The Second Reading for the 32nd Sunday of Ordinary Time

May our Lord Jesus Christ himself, and God our Father who has given us his love and, through his grace, such inexhaustible comfort and such sure hope, comfort you and strengthen you in everything good that you do or say.

Finally, brothers, pray for us; pray that the Lord's message may spread quickly, and be received with honour as it was among you; and pray that we may be preserved from the interference of bigoted and evil people, for faith is not given to everyone. But the Lord is faithful, and he will give you strength and guard you from the evil one, and we, in the Lord, have every confidence that you are doing and will go on doing all that we tell you. May the Lord turn your hearts towards the love of God and the fortitude of Christ.

2 Thessalonians 2:16 - 3:5

The words of Paul offer great consolation, as they reassure us of the tender love that was initially poured into our hearts though the Holy Spirit at our baptism for 'he first loved us' (1John 4:19). While Christ drew us first into himself at our baptism, 'the Eucharist reinforces that incorporation' (Ecclesia de Eucharistia, 23). In a spiritual sense, (that is, in our hearts) through our participation in the Eucharist, we are once again wrapped in the white baptismal garment that symbolises that we have 'put on Christ'. We share in his life so that he can comfort us and strengthen us in everything good that we do and say.

Just as Paul spoke of God's love, Pope Benedict XVI has written about this 'gift that Jesus Christ makes of himself, thus revealing God's infinite love for every man and woman. This wondrous sacrament, [the Holy Eucharist] makes manifest that "greater" love which led him to "lay down his life for his friends"' (SC, 1).

Where in my daily life do I encounter the love of God? Where in my daily life do I have an opportunity to show the love of God – to walk in charity and peace?

Prayer

Our closing prayer today is the Blessing which may have been used by the priest at the end of Mass on Sunday. In praying the words today, you might find it helpful to change the pronoun from 'you' or 'your' to 'me' and 'mine' or 'us' and 'our':

May almighty God bless you in his mercy,
and make you always aware of his saving wisdom.
Amen.
May he strengthen your faith with proofs of his love,
so that you will persevere in good works.
Amen.
May he direct your steps to himself,
and show you how to walk in charity and peace.
Amen.

Roman Missal, Solemn Blessing for Ordinary Time III

Pray that the Lord's message may spread quickly, and be received with honour as it was among you...

2 Thessalonians 3:1

We are frequently targeted by people who wish to sell us things, or wish us to make use of their services: their adverts pack out our magazines and newspapers; we see posters on street corners, and watch commercials on television and in the cinema. We too have a message to proclaim. Of necessity, our individual proclamation of the faith will be more modest. Yet, by our words and actions, we can demonstrate an authenticity more convincing than any advert or commercial.

Like St. Paul, who was anxious to spread the Lord's message, Pope Benedict XVI explains that the Good News is not to be jealously guarded; 'for the love that we celebrate in the sacrament [of the Eucharist] is not something that we can keep to ourselves. By its very nature it demands to be shared by all. Truly nothing is more beautiful than to know Christ and to make him known to others' (SC, 84).

How often do we stop to consider the power and, indeed, the potential of our words and actions?

Prayer

In the Penitential Rite, which may have been used at Mass on Sunday, we remember the way the Lord serves us. Sometimes we receive his gifts and use them well. Sometimes we neglect them. The rite has us remember his goodness, and entrust ourselves to his mercy. His love is our hope.

Lord Jesus, you have shown us the way to the Father:
Lord, have mercy

Lord Jesus, you have given us the consolation of the truth:
Christ, have mercy

Lord Jesus, you are the Good Shepherd:
Lord, have mercy

Roman Missal, Order of Mass, Penitential Rite c vii

> We, in the Lord, have every confidence that you are doing and will go on doing all that we tell you. May the Lord turn your hearts towards the love of God and the fortitude of Christ.
>
> *2 Thessalonians 3:4-5*

Through the celebration of the Eucharist, we enter into the very dynamic of Christ's self-giving. Through our common priesthood (by our baptism), our daily sacrifices made in love of others are mixed with Christ's Sacrifice made in love of all. We are empowered by the gift of God's love and invited to be bearers of that love to others.

As we consider the situation of those in our families, communities and indeed the world at large, we are aware of so much that could be done. There are people in need of the gifts of friendship and a listening ear; there are those who need help to develop life skills, for their own sake and the sake of their families; there are those who suffer because of the lack of other basic human needs.

None of us can respond to all of these needs, alone. But through mutual support, as today's extract from 2 Thessalonians suggests, together we can do much more. Within our parish family, doubtless, there will be many individuals doing what they can, responding to the particular situations they encounter. And, doubtless, members of our parish family will be active in organisations which help us coordinate our response to the needs of others - Catholic organisations and organisations formed by people of good will, whatever their faith. As members of the Body of Christ, we are joined with others and together we are asked to do much more than we can do on our own.

As a community how do we respond to the needs of others in our families, communities and in the wider world?

From Sacramentum Caritatis

76. The eucharistic form of Christian life is clearly an ecclesial and communitarian form. Through the Diocese and the parish, the fundamental structures of the Church in a particular territory, each individual believer can experience concretely what it means to be a member of Christ's Body. Associations, ecclesial movements and new communities – with their lively charisms bestowed by the Holy Spirit for the needs of our time – together with Institutes of Consecrated Life, have a particular responsibility for helping to make the faithful conscious that they belong to the Lord (cf. Romans 14:8). Secularisation, with its inherent emphasis on individualism, has its most negative effects on individuals who are isolated and lack a sense of belonging. Christianity, from its very beginning, has meant fellowship, a network of relationships constantly strengthened by hearing God's Word and sharing in the Eucharist, and enlivened by the Holy Spirit.

Prayer

God of mercy,
in the Eucharist we proclaim the death of the Lord.
Accept the gifts we present
and help us follow him with love,
for he is Lord for ever and ever.
Amen.

Roman Missal, Prayer over the Gifts for 32nd Sunday of the Year

Remember, Lord, your people

When we celebrate the Mass we celebrate as Church, not just as individuals, but as a community, as a family, made one in Christ. At the heart of all that we do and believe is the conviction that the well being of our community, indeed of any family, is dependent upon its being united to Christ. It is not surprising therefore that Pope John Paul II pointed to the Eucharist as the very source of Christian marriage in his Apostolic Exhortation *Familiaris Consortio*. In the Eucharist, where Christ's complete self-offering is re-presented to us, we see the origins of the marriage covenant and the living we are called to in all the sacraments.

The full extent of our 'family', the community, is recalled in the Eucharistic Prayer where in union with the angels and the saints we pray for the living and the dead; for ourselves and for those who have gone before us marked with the sign of faith. In terms of those who have gone before us the Eucharistic Prayer is an opportunity to pray for them. For us, who still strive, it affords us the opportunity to invoke the prayers of the saints in whom, as Pope John Paul II puts it in *Ecclesia de Eucharistia*, the Eucharist took on the splendour of a lived reality (EE, 62).

Prayer

For your daily prayer today, pray the following words from
Eucharistic Prayer I – a prayer which helps us deepen our awareness
and love for the community of the Church.

Commemoration of the living
Remember, Lord, your people, especially those for whom we now pray,
Remember all of us gathered here before you.
You know how firmly we believe in you and dedicate ourselves to you.
We offer you this sacrifice of praise for ourselves and those who are dear to us.
We pray to you, our living and true God, for our well-being and redemption.

Commemoration of the dead
Remember, Lord, those who have died and have gone before us marked
with the sign of faith, especially those for whom we now pray. May these,
and all who sleep in Christ, find in your presence light, happiness,
and peace.

The Saints
For ourselves, too, we ask
some share in the fellowship of your apostles and martyrs,
with John the Baptist, Stephen, Matthias, Barnabas,
[Ignatius, Alexander, Marcellinus, Peter,
Felicity, Perpetua, Agatha, Lucy, Agnes, Cecilia, Anastasia] and all the saints.
Though we are sinners, we trust in your mercy and love.
Do not consider what we truly deserve, but grant us your forgiveness.

From Roman Missal, Eucharistic Prayer I, (paras 81, 97, 98)

The Gospel for 33rd Sunday in Ordinary Time

When some were talking about the Temple, remarking how it was adorned with fine stonework and votive offerings, Jesus said, 'All these things you are staring at now - the time will come when not a single stone will be left on another: everything will be destroyed.' And they put to him this question: 'Master,' they said, 'when will this happen, then, and what sign will there be that this is about to take place?'

'Take care not to be deceived,' he said, 'because many will come using my name and saying, "I am he" and, "The time is near at hand." Refuse to join them. And when you hear of wars and revolutions, do not be frightened, for this is something that must happen but the end is not soon.' Then he said to them, 'Nation will fight against nation, and kingdom against kingdom. There will be great earthquakes and plagues and famines here and there; there will be fearful sights and great signs from heaven.

'But before all this happens, men will seize you and persecute you; they will hand you over to the synagogues and to imprisonment, and bring you before kings and governors because of my name - and that will be your opportunity to bear witness. Keep this carefully in mind: you are not to prepare your defence, because I myself shall give you an eloquence and a wisdom that none of your opponents will be able to resist or contradict. You will be betrayed even by parents and brothers, relations and friends; and some of you will be put to death. You will be hated by all men on account of my name, but not a hair of your head will be lost. Your endurance will win you your lives.'

Luke 21:5-19

St. Luke is believed to have written his gospel in the latter stages of the first century while he was working to build up the Church in Asia Minor (present day Turkey). In this particular passage, he recounts how Jesus foretold the destruction of the Temple in Jerusalem (which took place in 70 AD) and the persecution that Luke's contemporaries would undergo for the sake of their Christianity.

St. Luke also records Jesus' speaking of his Second Coming; his glorious return which scholars often refer to as the Parousia. Soon we will be entering into the season of Advent where the initial emphasis will be on Christ's Second Coming, rather than his birth in Bethlehem. The early Christians expected Christ to return fairly quickly, but as Christ says, the end was not to be so soon. 'Until that day, the Church', as St Augustine puts it, 'progresses on her pilgrimage amidst the world's persecutions and God's consolations' (Catechism of the Catholic Church, 769). Christ's word for us, in the midst of this pilgrimage, is clear; do not be frightened, keep faithful, persevere. 'Your endurance will win you your lives'. Indeed, it is not the bricks and mortar of any building or temple that will be there to protect us, but Christ himself. 'I myself', he says, 'shall give you an eloquence and a wisdom that none of your opponents will be able to resist or contradict'.

What troubles my mind or life at this time? What wisdom does the Lord offer me to help me to enter into the peace he gives?

Prayer

The Lord blesses any situation, even the most distressing. In the Eucharistic Prayer we remember the way in which Jesus passed through death to life, redeeming the hopeless. In our daily prayer we can bring every situation to the Lord, in hope and faith.

Through Christ our Lord
you give us all these gifts.
You fill them with life and goodness,
you bless them and make them holy.

Roman Missal, Eucharistic Prayer I

Opening Prayer

Leader: O Lord, who may abide in your tent?
Who may dwell on your holy hill?

Group: **Those who walk blamelessly,
and do what is right,
and speak the truth from their heart;**

Leader: who do not slander with their tongue,
and do no evil to their friends,
nor take up a reproach against their neighbours;

Group: **in whose eyes the wicked are despised,
but who honour those who fear the Lord;**

Leader: who stand by their oath even to their hurt;
who do not lend money at interest,
and do not take a bribe against the innocent.

Group: **Those who do these things
shall never be moved.**

All: **Glory be to the Father...**

Psalm 15

After a short silence, the group or an individual says:

Come then, good Shepherd, bread divine,
still show to us thy mercy sign;
oh, feed us, still keep us thine;
so we may see thy glories shine
in fields of immortality.
O thou, the wisest, mightiest, best,
our present food, our future rest,
come, make us each thy chosen guest,
co-heirs of thine, and comrades blest
with saints whose dwelling is with thee.

St. Thomas Aquinas (1225-1274)

Explore the Sunday Scriptures for the 33rd Sunday in Ordinary Time Luke 21: 5 – 19

When some were talking about the Temple, remarking how it was adorned with fine stonework and votive offerings, Jesus said, 'All these things you are staring at now – the time will come when not a single stone will be left on another: everything will be destroyed.' And they put to him this question: 'Master,' they said 'when will this happen, then, and what sign will there be that this is about to take place?'

'Take care not to be deceived,' he said 'because many will come using my name and saying, "I am he" and, "The time is near at hand". Refuse to join them. And when you hear of wars and revolutions, do not be frightened, for this is something that must happen but the end is not so soon.' Then he said to them, 'Nation will fight against nation, and kingdom against kingdom. There will be great earthquakes and plagues and famines here and there; there will be fearful sights and great signs from heaven.

'But before all this happens, men will seize you and persecute you; they will hand you over to the synagogues and imprisonment, and bring you before kings and governors because of my name – and that will be your opportunity to bear witness. Keep this carefully in mind: you are not to prepare your defence, because I myself shall give you an eloquence and a wisdom that none of your opponents will be able to resist or contradict. You will be betrayed even by parents and brothers, relations and friends; and some of you will be put to death. You will be hated by all men on account of my name, but not a hair of your heard will be lost. Your endurance will win you your lives.

Following a short period of silence you may wish to share an image, a thought, a phrase, a question that has struck you.

For Reflection

St. Luke recounted Christ's prophetic teaching – that humankind would be confronted by natural disasters and politically driven turmoil of such magnitude as to cause both mass destruction and great human loss. Yet, we are counselled not to be afraid - for Christ will always be with us.

In previous weeks' meditations, we have contemplated the celebration of the Eucharist. While the Liturgy of the Word offers us direction as to how we are to live our daily lives in imitation of Christ, we are strengthened for our life's journey through the gift of his body in Holy Communion. Although the eucharistic celebration may have ended, we are not left to our own devices. The consecrated bread and wine known as 'the Real Presence' or 'the Blessed Sacrament' aren't placed in the tabernacle towards the end of Mass simply for convenient storage. On the contrary, Christ is with us at all times and we have what might best be described as 'a standing invitation' from Christ to spend some time with him during the course of our week. Somewhere in the darkened church, a red candle will be burning to indicate his Real Presence.

By extending his hospitality, Christ is offering each of us much more than a listening ear for our prayers and petitions. We are being invited to deepen our personal relationship with him. While the idea of dialogue with our transcendent God may initially seem rather unnatural, when we think of other close relationships, non-verbal communication is often the norm. People generally cherish the quiet moments spent with loved ones when unspoken thoughts are frequently exchanged and great comfort felt simply by another's presence. Even very young children quickly grow to understand the meaning conveyed solely by a look on their parent's face.

Undoubtedly, it takes time to develop a level of comfort and familiarity that enables one to connect at this level but Christ is waiting for each of us and hoping that we will want to get to know him better. By spending quiet time before the Blessed Sacrament, gazing at the tabernacle or monstrance, we can begin to feel Christ's intimate presence within our being; to sense our connection with his Paschal Mystery and to recognise his mission as a framework for our day-to-day living. Rather than readily accepting society's current tendency to focus on the individual and personal choices, our perspective may become more a matter of 'we' as we come to understand that Christ, with whom we were joined at baptism, is with us always.

Amidst the demands of everyday life, the invitation to spend some quiet time with Christ - before the Blessed Sacrament - can easily be overlooked but if we think of the trouble he has gone to on our behalf - how can we ignore it?

Share your thoughts on this reflection. How does this week's Scripture reading and reflection encourage, affirm or challenge you? What impact might this have on your daily living? To bring this period of sharing to an end the following extract may be useful.

From Sacramentum Caritatis

68. The personal relationship which the individual believer establishes with Jesus present in the Eucharist constantly points beyond itself to the whole communion of the Church and nourishes a fuller sense of membership in the Body of Christ.

Leader: Aloud or in the silence of our hearts let us bring to the Father our thanks (pause)…

Leader: In sorrow let us ask the Father for forgiveness (pause)…

Leader: With confidence let us entrust to the Father our cares and concerns (pause)…

Prayer

Almighty God,
help us to encourage one another to walk joyfully,
our hearts filled with wonder,
towards our encounter with the Holy Eucharist,
so that we may experience and proclaim to others
the truth of the words with which Jesus took leave of his disciples:
'Lo, I am with you always, until the end of the world'.
Amen.

Adapted from Sacramentum Caritatis, 97

help us to experience the salvation you won for us

Over the past weeks our focus has been on our participation in Mass. This week our focus is on the worship of the Eucharist outside of Mass, something encouraged to be a regular feature of parish life by Cardinal Cormac Murphy-O'Connor.

Even when we celebrate Mass in the most worthy fashion, with times of silence and reflection, there will always be more to the Mass than we can focus on in prayer there and then. Of course, these are things we can ponder on, pray to the Lord about, any time and anywhere. But there is a particular value in offering this prayer in the presence of the Blessed Sacrament. There, we have the privilege of offering our prayer in the presence of the Lord himself, really and truly present in the reserved Sacrament.

What time, each week, could I spend in prayer before the Blessed Sacrament?

From Sacramentum Caritatis

66. The inherent relationship between Mass and adoration of the Blessed Sacrament was not always perceived with sufficient clarity. For example, an objection that was widespread at the time argued that the eucharistic bread was given to us not to be looked at, but to be eaten. In the light of the Church's experience of prayer, however, this was seen to be a false dichotomy. As Saint Augustine put it: 'no one eats that flesh without first adoring it; we should sin were we not to adore it.' In the Eucharist, the Son of God comes to meet us and desires to become one with us; eucharistic adoration is simply the natural consequence of the eucharistic celebration, which is itself the Church's supreme act of

adoration... The act of adoration outside Mass prolongs and intensifies all that takes place during the liturgical celebration itself. Indeed, 'only in adoration can a profound and genuine reception mature. And it is precisely this personal encounter with the Lord that then strengthens the social mission contained in the Eucharist, which seeks to break down not only the walls that separate the Lord and ourselves, but also and especially the walls that separate us from one another.'

Prayer

Lord Jesus Christ,
you gave us the eucharist
as the memorial of your suffering and death.
May our worship of this sacrament of your body and blood
help us to experience the salvation you won for us
and the peace of the kingdom
where you live with the Father and the Holy Spirit,
one God for ever and ever.
Amen.

Rite of Eucharistic Exposition and Benediction, Prayer before Blessing I

Father in heaven,
ever-living source of all that is good,
from the beginning of time you promised man salvation
through the future coming of your Son, our Lord Jesus Christ.
Help us to drink of his truth
and expand our hearts with the joy of his promises,
so that we may serve you in faith and in love
and know for ever the joy of your presence.

Roman Missal, Alternative Opening Prayer for 33rd Sunday in Ordinary Time

There is such richness in Scripture. All of life is there, from pain and death to joy, praise and life. One of the riches of liturgical prayer, and particularly of the Mass, is that it has its own drive, direction and content. We do not have to worry about which passages of Scripture we might read today - the Lectionary sets the texts before us. We do not have to decide which aspect of the Lord's life and ministry to bring to our prayer and reflection; by and large the seasons of the liturgical year look after that matter.

Through the liturgy, which we all share in together, the Lord finds ways to speak directly and personally to each one of us. In the prayer above, which may have been used at Mass yesterday, we pray for this. That said, there are also times when we ourselves need to set the agenda, bringing to the Lord those things which trouble us, or which bring us particular joy. Prayer before the Blessed Sacrament gives us space and a privileged opportunity for such prayer.

Prayer

This prayer, one of those offered by the Church for use at Exposition of the Blessed Sacrament, expresses beautifully the life-giving power of Christ's gift of himself in the Eucharist.

You are the Bread of life: Alleluia!
You are the Bread of salvation: Alleluia!
You are the Blood that redeemed us: Alleluia!
You are the source of our joy: Alleluia!
You are the Bread that feeds us: Alleluia!
You are the Blood that quenches our thirst: Alleluia!
You are the Bread that comforts us: Alleluia!
You are the Bread that gives us strength: Alleluia!
You are the Bread that heals us in body and mind: Alleluia! Alleluia! Alleluia!

Holy Communion and Worship of the Eucharist outside Mass,
Supplementary Appendix

The Second Reading for 33rd Sunday in Ordinary Time

You know how you are supposed to imitate us: now we were not idle when we were with you, nor did we ever have our meals at anyone's table without paying for them; no, we worked night and day, slaving and straining, so as not to be a burden on any of you. This was not because we had no right to be, but in order to make ourselves an example for you to follow.

We gave you a rule when we were with you: not to let anyone have any food if he refused to do any work. Now we hear that there are some of you who are living in idleness, doing no work themselves but interfering with everyone else's. In the Lord Jesus Christ, we order and call on people of this kind to go on quietly working and earning the food that they eat.

2 Thessalonians 3:7-12

For many of us, our lives revolve around activities of one kind or another. Even as young children we may have been told not to waste time – idleness. Finding time and actually spending it in contemplation before the Blessed Sacrament may, therefore, be viewed as countercultural, even 'foreign'.

While it's definitely a challenge to turn our minds away from 'earthly' thoughts, Christ invites us to spend more time with him than the hour or so of the Sunday liturgy. Why? Because he loves us! He wants to have a personal relationship with each one of us. If our time with Christ is but a fleeting moment, how can we respond to his love and hospitality? As with every valued friendship, it needs time and effort to grow. We can get to know Christ better by spending time in silence before the Real Presence to contemplate his mystery. As Mother Theresa said: 'If we really want to pray, we must first learn to listen, for in the silence of the heart – God speaks'.

How much silence is there in my prayer? Do I take time to listen to God? Is my prayer filled with my speaking?

Prayer

In this Responsory, another of the prayers offered for use during Exposition, we recall the promises of the Lord: that in him we will have life.

The living Father has sent me and I have life from the Father.
He who eats me, has life from me.
The Lord has fed him on the bread of life and understanding.
He who eats me has life from me.

Holy Communion and Worship of the Eucharist outside Mass, Appendix

We gave you a rule when we were with you....

2 Thessalonians 3:10

Many organisations, develop a mission statement. Many people develop a rule of life for themselves. St. Paul, for example, tells us that he has taken Jesus as a model, a 'rule', for his life.

When we come before the Blessed Sacrament for prayer and worship, we are confronted by the way that Jesus 'gives himself away' in love for us. He is re-presented to us in the form of bread that is broken, in the form of wine that is shared. And it would be surprising if at the meal celebrated in memory of him, we did not also call to mind the mystery of service that St. John relates in his gospel, the Washing of the Feet. The Eucharist and the Washing of the Feet are two principal ways in which the 'rule' of Jesus is set before us. Other moments in Jesus' life also impress themselves on us, and set before us the pattern that we wish to follow. Prayer is an opportunity to reflect on these moments and ask for the grace to grow in holiness of life.

Prayer

In this Responsory we are invited to make full use of our senses to draw our minds and hearts into our act of worship.

See in this bread the body that hung on the cross;
see in this cup the blood that flowed from his side.
Take and eat the body of Christ; take and drink his blood.
For now you are members of Christ.
Receive the bond of love and be united;
receive the price of your salvation and know your worth.
For now you are members of Christ.
Holy Communion and Worship of the Eucharist outside Mass, Appendix

Go on quietly working...

2 Thessalonians 3:12

Sometimes it can seem that so much is asked of us as Christians. We can take consolation from St. Paul who calls us not to something extraordinary, but to show that we are Christ-like in the way we carry out the ordinary things of life.

It is through the offering up to God of these 'ordinary' things of life, by 'quietly working' that we respond to Christ's love. In everyday acts we are presented with opportunities to show love and caring, yet these moments are often missed. In moments of silence, of thought, of contemplation and prayer we are able to reflect on our 'vocation', on how the 'ordinary' things that we do and say help others see God. When Jesus washed the feet of his disciples, an act typical of that time and place, he showed his love for them. By simply playing our part with love we are doing what we are called to do as Christians. Christ calls us to this way of life, and he offers us the grace we need to respond.

Prayer

This further Responsory invites us to dwell on the communion of the Church, born of our sharing in the Eucharist.

We though many are one bread, one body;
for we all share one bread and one cup.
You have made us live in peace in your house, O Lord;
in your kindness you have prepared a banquet for the poor,
for we all share one bread and one cup.

Holy Communion and Worship of the Eucharist outside Mass, Appendix

Father, all-powerful and ever-living God,
we do well always and everywhere to give you thanks
through Jesus Christ our Lord.
By his birth we are reborn.
In his suffering we are freed from sin.
By his rising from the dead we rise to ever-lasting life.
In his return to you in glory
we enter into your heavenly kingdom.
And so we join the angels and the saints
as they sing their unending hymn of praise:
Holy…

Roman Missal, Order of Mass, Preface of Sunday in Ordinary Time IV

The mystery of our salvation is one that we can never exhaust. One of its most extraordinary features is the way in which Christ draws us into a most profound communion of life with him. In the Preface above, which may have been used at Mass on Sunday, we are reminded how through the various events of Jesus' life, we are brought to new life. By his taking our humanity to himself, he opens to us the opportunity to share in his divinity.

This invitation to intimacy is of course made all the more clear to us in the sharing of sacramental communion. The Lord gives himself over to us, so that we might make a gift of ourselves to him. As if this was not enough, we are assured that this communion with Jesus which we share today, extends beyond the here and now into the glory of heaven.

Prayer

This final prayer is one of those that may be used before Benediction.
It reminds us that the Eucharist is given to renew our lives.

Lord our God,
teach us to cherish in our hearts
the paschal mystery of your Son
by which you redeemed the world.
Watch over the gifts of grace
your love has given us
and bring them to fulfilment
in the glory of heaven.
We ask this through Christ our Lord.
Amen.

Rite of Eucharistic Exposition and Benediction, Prayer before Blessing, 7

The Gospel for the Solemnity of Christ the King

The people stayed there before the cross watching Jesus. As for the leaders, they jeered at him. 'He saved others,' they said, 'let him save himself if he is the Christ of God, the Chosen One.' The soldiers mocked him too, and when they approached to offer him vinegar they said, 'If you are the king of the Jews, save yourself.' Above him there was an inscription: 'This is the King of the Jews.' One of the criminals hanging there abused him. 'Are you not the Christ?' he said. 'Save yourself and us as well.' But the other spoke up and rebuked him. 'Have you no fear of God at all?' he said. 'You got the same sentence as he did, but in our case we deserved it: we are paying for what we did. But this man has done nothing wrong. Jesus,' he said, 'remember me when you come into your kingdom.' 'Indeed, I promise you,' he replied, 'today you will be with me in paradise.'

Luke 23:35-43

Over the past six weeks we have reflected on the way in which the Lord invites us to share in his life through our participation in the liturgy. In the gospel we will hear tomorrow we hear again how freely and generously that gift is given.

While on the Cross, Jesus promised the repentant thief that he will attain final rest in God's kingdom. This same promise is made to us. If we respond to the love poured out, much as the blood and cleansing water flowed from the side of Christ, we will see God. The season of Advent is almost upon us, a season of preparation for Christ's coming, his first, but also a season where remember that he will come again. The Sacrament of the Eucharist is a foretaste of the Second Coming and our sharing in the heavenly banquet (Matthew 26:29).

Grace is freely given to all who have need, and are willing to receive. Throughout the season of Advent and, indeed, the rest of our lives, how great should be our thanksgiving that Christ's promises to us are so generously fulfilled, that we are able to share in his life?

Prayer

Our final prayer is a Meditation Prayer offered for use during Exposition. It forms a fitting conclusion to the meditation and prayer which has been at the heart of *Sharing in His Life*.

We share in the gift of Christ's body,
given to us in the form of bread,
given to us for all time.
This food from heaven
brings us together in unity
as parts of the one body of Christ.
In this sacrament
we are drawn to share in God's life,
a foretaste of the glory of heaven.

Father,
our human words are not enough to thank you...
our human minds cannot penetrate this mystery...
Open our hearts to sing your praises...
open our minds to your Spirit of wisdom and love...
Help us to know that we are one...
Show us the way to be more closely united in you,
through your Son whose body and blood we eat and drink,
through the love and the fire of the Spirit.
Amen.

Holy Communion and Worship of the Eucharist
outside Mass, Supplementary Appendix

Notes